the Cooking Light
Gluten-Free cookbook

Simple Food Solutions
for Everyday Meals

D0507234

ISBN-13: 978-0-8487-3435-0
ISBN-10: 0-8487-3435-1
Library of Congress Control Number: 2010936021

Printed in the United States of America
First Printing 2011

Oxmoor House

VP, Publishing Director: Jim Childs
Editorial Director: Susan Payne Dobbs
Brand Manager: Michelle Turner Aycock
Senior Editor: Heather Averett
Managing Editor: Laurie S. Herr

The Cooking Light® Gluten-Free Cookbook

Editors: Andrea C. Kirkland, MS, RD;
Rachel Quinlivan West, RD
Project Editor: Diane Rose
Senior Designer: Emily Albright Parrish
Director, Test Kitchens: Elizabeth Tyler Austin
Assistant Directors,
Test Kitchens: Julie Christopher, Julie Gunter
Test Kitchens Professionals: Wendy Ball, Allison E. Cox, Victoria E. Cox, Margaret Monroe Dickey, Alyson Moreland Haynes, Stefanie Maloney, Callie Nash, Catherine Crowell Steele, Ashley T. Strickland, Leah Van Deren
Photography Director: Jim Bathie
Senior Photo Stylist: Kay E. Clarke
Associate Photo Stylist: Katherine Eckert Coyne
Assistant Photo Stylist: Mary Louise Menendez
Production Manager: Theresa Beste-Farley

Contributors

Designer: Blair Gillespie
Culinary Consultant: Carol Fenster, PhD
Copy Editor: Jasmine Hodges
Proofreader: Norma Butterworth-McKittrick
Indexer: Mary Ann Laurens
Recipe Developers: Wendy Cruze; Carol Fenster, PhD; Carol Kicinski
Nutrition Analysis: Caroline Glagola, Kate Grigsby
Interns: Erin Bishop, Sarah H. Doss, Alison Loughman, Rita A. Omokha, Lindsay A. Rozier, Caitlin Watzke
Test Kitchens Professional: Kathleen Royal Phillips
Photographers: Becky Luigart-Stayner, Mary Britton Senseney
Photo Stylists: Missie Neville Crawford, Lydia DeGaris Pursell, Leslie Simpson

Time Home Entertainment Inc.

Publisher: Richard Fraiman
General Manager: Steven Sandonato
Executive Director,
Marketing Services: Carol Pittard
Executive Director,
Retail & Special Sales: Tom Mifsud
Director,
New Product Development: Peter Harper
Director, Bookazine
Development & Marketing: Laura Adam
Assistant Director,
Brand Marketing: Joy Butts
Associate Counsel: Helen Wan

Cooking Light®

Editor: Scott Mowbray
Creative Director: Carla Frank
Deputy Editor: Phillip Rhodes
Executive Editor, Food: Ann Taylor Pittman
Special Publications Editor: Mary Simpson Creel, MS, RD
Senior Food Editor: Julianna Grimes
Senior Editor: Cindy Hatcher
Associate Food Editor: Timothy Q. Cebula
Assistant Editors: Kimberly Hollard, Phoebe Wu
Test Kitchen Director: Vanessa T. Pruett
Assistant Test
Kitchen Director: Tiffany Vickers Davis
Recipe Testers
and Developers: Robin Bashinsky, Adam Hickman, Deb Wise
Art Director: Fernande Bondarenko
Junior Deputy Art Director: Alexander Spacher
Associate Art Director: Rachel Lasserre
Designer: Chase Turberville
Photo Director: Kristen Schaefer
Assistant Photo Editor: Amy Delaune
Senior Photographer: Randy Mayor
Senior Photo Stylist: Cindy Barr
Photo Stylist: Leigh Ann Ross
Chief Food Stylist: Charlotte Autry
Senior Food Stylist: Kellie Gerber Kelley
Copy Chief: Maria Parker Hopkins
Assistant Copy Chief: Susan Roberts
Research Editor: Michelle Gibson Daniels
Editorial Production
Director: Liz Rhoades
Production Editor: Hazel R. Eddins
Assistant Production Editor: Josh Rutledge
Administrative Coordinator: Carol D. Johnson
CookingLight.com Editor: Allison Long Lowery
CookingLight.com
Nutrition Editor: Holley Johnson Grainger, MS, RD
Production Assistant: Mallory Daugherty

To order additional publications, call 1-800-765-6400 or 1-800-491-0551.

For more books to enrich your life, visit **oxmoorhouse.com**

To search, savor, and share thousands of recipes, visit **myrecipes.com**

Front cover: Pepperoni Pizza, page 164

Back cover: Diner-Style Onion Rings, page 48; Mocha Cream Brownie Wedges with Fresh Raspberries, page 256

the Cooking Light
Gluten-Free
cookbook

Oxmoor
House

Contents

Welcome

For the millions of you on a gluten-free diet, food is vitally important. When you follow a special diet, what you eat keeps you healthy (or doesn't) and can have a great effect on how you feel day to day. But, like everyone else who doesn't have to eat gluten free, your lives are busy and hectic, and preparing healthy meals is just another item on your to-do list. That's where this book comes in. When creating *The Cooking Light Gluten-Free Cookbook,* our goal was simple: to bring you healthy, great-tasting food that you can eat. In this book, we did just that.

Gluten free doesn't mean flavor free, and we made sure to include all of your favorite foods—from pizzas and pastas to muffins and cakes. You'll find many of the things you crave in the pages of this book. To help you succeed in meal planning and following a gluten-free lifestyle, we have made substitutions for ingredients in more than 150 *Cooking Light* recipes and transformed them into delicious gluten-free recipes that you and your family can enjoy.

The *Cooking Light* Editors

Gluten-Free Kitchen

what is gluten?

Gluten is something many people don't worry about, but for those who must follow a diet without it, avoiding it is top priority. Here's what you need to know to understand exactly which foods to avoid.

the culprit

Technically, gluten is the general name for specific proteins found in wheat, barley, and rye. Most people can eat gluten with no ill effects, but gluten is toxic for several million others.

who needs to go gluten free?

A gluten-free diet is required for individuals diagnosed with celiac disease, gluten sensitivity, and wheat allergies and is sometimes recommended for children with autism.

Celiac disease is a digestive disorder in which gluten damages the lining of the small intestine and reduces its ability to absorb vital nutrients. It is an autoimmune condition rather than a food allergy because gluten-containing food actually causes damage to the lining of the small intestine. This damage increases the risk of malnutrition because the small intestine can't effectively absorb nutrients. Common symptoms include diarrhea, constipation, gas, bloating, weight loss, nausea, vitamin deficiencies, and severe abdominal pain, but gluten can also cause further damage and additional symptoms in other areas of the body. The range and severity of symptoms varies greatly among individuals, and the level of gluten in certain foods affects each person differently. The only treatment is a lifelong gluten-free diet.

Persons with gluten sensitivity can exhibit a wide range of reactions, from digestive issues to headaches, balance problems, and many other difficulties. And these symptoms may range from mild to severe. The only treatment for gluten sensitivity is avoidance of gluten.

Individuals with allergies must avoid wheat proteins, which include gluten. Symptoms can include hives, nasal congestion, nausea, and anaphylaxis. The only treatment is avoidance of wheat products.

Some physicians prescribe a diet free of gluten and casein (a milk protein) to improve behavior in children with autism. Not all autistic children respond to a gluten-free/casein-free diet (known as a GFCF diet), and it is typically used as a part of the overall treatment.

lactose intolerance

Many people who cannot eat gluten also experience lactose intolerance—gluten-induced damage to the intestines can decrease the ability to digest lactose. For the recipes in this book containing dairy products, you can make ingredient substitutions using dairy-free plain yogurts and cheeses, dairy-free buttery spreads in place of butter, and dairy-free beverages such as plain rice, soy, coconut, or hemp milk in place of cow's milk. Please note that these products often have different textures and flavors compared to their dairy-containing counterparts, so you may need to experiment with the recipes to get the results you like.

what to do now

Gluten is everywhere and shows up in some unexpected places, including many prepackaged and processed foods, but that doesn't mean you can't enjoy a big plate of pasta or a slice of pizza ever again. In the following pages, we'll expand on how to stock a gluten-free pantry; identify unexpected sources of gluten; and determine which foods are safe to eat, those to avoid, and those to question. You will also learn how to become a successful gluten-free baker; shop smart; decode food labels; and stay safe in the kitchen so you can prepare delicious and healthy gluten-free meals.

stocking a gluten-free kitchen

This process begins in the grocery store. It requires careful label reading and a keen awareness of cross-contamination issues that can put naturally gluten-free foods on the do-not-eat list.

Label reading is a vital part of creating a gluten-free kitchen (we'll show you more on page 22), and if a label isn't clear or you're uncertain, then you'll need to contact the manufacturer to find out more. It's always better to be safe than sick.

This chapter is divided into three major sections: foods that are safe to eat, foods to avoid, and foods to question. The information on the following pages isn't meant to be an all-inclusive list, but rather a general overview. For more information, there are a number of online resources to visit:

- celiac.org (Celiac Disease Foundation)
- americanceliac.org (American Celiac Disease Alliance)
- gluten.net (Gluten Intolerance Group of North America)
- celiaccentral.org (National Foundation for Celiac Awareness)
- glutenfreeliving.com (*Gluten-Free Living* magazine)
- livingwithout.com (*Living Without* magazine)
- csaceliacs.org (Celiac Sprue Association)

sources of gluten

label requirements

Since 2006, food manufacturers have been required to identify foods that contain any of the eight major allergenic foods, including wheat and all of its derivatives (example: spelt), on food labels. (The others are milk, eggs, fish, crustacean shellfish, tree nuts, peanuts, and soy.) This labeling requirement makes identifying gluten-free foods easier because wheat is the bulk of what you're trying to avoid. If wheat is used as an ingredient, the ingredient list must clearly state "wheat," in these words: "Contains: Wheat."

cross-contamination

Another unexpected source of gluten and a very common reason for naturally gluten-free foods to contain gluten is cross-contamination, both in your home (see page 24 for information about keeping your kitchen safe) and by food manufacturers during processing, storage, and transport. Cross-contamination can occur at many points—at the farm if both gluten-free and gluten-containing grains are grown in close proximity, at food-manufacturing plants if the grain is processed on machinery where a gluten-containing grain was also processed and the line wasn't thoroughly cleaned, and if the grains were stored near each other. The only way you can be assured a grain is truly gluten free is if the manufacturer tests for gluten or if it has been grown, harvested, milled, stored, and packaged in a facility that exclusively grows and processes gluten-free food. It is also best to avoid buying any foods or ingredients (such as flour or grains) in bulk bins because they may be cross-contaminated from inappropriate handling by employees or customers.

oats

Oats are naturally gluten free but are easily susceptible to cross-contamination. Oats are often rotated in the fields with gluten-containing grains, which means they can be contaminated in the field and during transport. However, several companies now offer pure, uncontaminated oats that contain no gluten, so look for these gluten-free oats in stores or online.

gluten-free products

Numerous gluten-free products are available in stores and online—from baking mixes and flours to pizza doughs and pastas—and new products are added all the time. While many gluten-free products, like sauces and condiments, can be used interchangeably in the same way that their gluten-containing counterparts can, some can't and need to be handled differently.

These are primarily products that normally contain gluten (breads, pastas, mixes, desserts) but have been made with gluten-free ingredients, which perform differently. For these products, be sure to reference the packages and use the cooking instructions specified for that product. Various brands of the same product can also act differently based on the mix of ingredients and the amounts of each ingredient they contain, so a procedure and cooking time that worked perfectly for quinoa pasta won't always work for rice pasta, and one pancake mix may have a different texture than another. Follow the package directions and our instructions in the recipes closely for the best results.

what to eat (and not eat)?

This list is not meant to be exhaustive, but rather an overview of common foods that are safe to eat, should be questioned, or should always be avoided. Always read the labels before making any food purchase.

safe to eat

- Amaranth
- Arrowroot
- Beans
- Buckwheat
- Chickpeas (garbanzo beans)
- Corn
- Cornstarch
- Eggs
- Fish and shellfish
- Flaxseed
- Fresh fruit
- Fresh vegetables
- Grits
- Hominy
- Lentils
- Meat
- Mesquite
- Milk
- Millet
- Montina™ (Indian ricegrass)
- Peas
- Polenta
- Potato starch and potato flour
- Potatoes
- Poultry
- Products labeled gluten free

- Quinoa
- Raw nuts
- Rice
- Sorghum
- Tapioca
- Teff

foods to check

These foods may be made with or without gluten, so it is important to read labels to find a safe version. By law, companies have to list wheat on the label if it is found in any ingredient.

- Baked goods like bread, breadcrumbs, cakes, cookies, croutons, muffins, and piecrusts
- Beer
- Bouillon
- Breading and coating mixes
- Broth (all varieties)
- Candy
- Cereal
- Coated popcorn and chips
- Corn tortillas
- Crackers
- Energy bars
- Fast food
- Flavored alcoholic drinks
- Flavored or coated nuts and seeds
- Flavored teas
- Gravies, marinades, and sauces
- Hoisin sauce
- Licorice
- Ice cream
- Imitation seafood
- Marinades
- Multigrain rice and corn cakes
- Oats (look for gluten-free oats)
- Pastas
- Pepperoni

- Prepackaged, convenience foods
- Prepared icings and frostings
- Prepared salsas
- Processed foods
- Processed meats (hot dogs, lunch meat, and sausage)
- Roasted nuts
- Rotisserie chicken
- Salad dressings
- Sauces and gravies
- Seasoned rice mixes
- Seasoning mixes
- Soups
- Soy sauce
- Spices (if there is no ingredient list on the label, then it contains only the pure spice)
- Teriyaki sauce
- Vegetables packaged with sauces
- Worcestershire sauce
- Yogurt (with granola)

foods to avoid

- Barley
- Barley malt
- Bran (oat, wheat)
- Bulgur
- Cooking spray for baking (may contain wheat flour)
- Couscous
- Durum
- Einkorn
- Emmer
- Farina
- Farro
- Flour containing wheat, barley, or rye or any of their derivatives
- Graham flour
- Hydrolyzed wheat protein
- Kamut
- Malted milk
- Malt flavorings

- Malt vinegar
- Matzo
- Meat, poultry, seafood, or vegetables that are breaded, floured, served with a sauce made from wheat, or marinated in a wheat-based sauce such as soy or teriyaki
- Rye
- Seitan
- Semolina
- Spelt
- Triticale
- Wheat
- Wheat germ

gluten-free baking

Baking can be one of the more challenging aspects of following a gluten-free diet. The reason: Gluten is created during the kneading process and gives breads their distinctive stretchy, elastic quality and structure.

gluten-free flours and baking mixes

Gluten-free flours lack elasticity. Plus, most gluten-free dough is sticky and doesn't lend itself to kneading by hand. But gluten-free baking has come a deliciously long way as more gluten-free flours and gums, such as xanthan gum and guar gum, have become available. These gums, eggs, egg whites, and leavening agents like baking powder and baking soda will create elasticity and structure and impart moisture to your baked goods. You'll find a small glossary of some of these products on page 18.

We found that gluten-free baking mixes behave differently. Each contains varying amounts of flour and leavening agents, and some are more finely ground than others. These differences naturally create variations in the final baked product. In these situations, we've included the name of the brand that yielded the best results. However, if you have a go-to gluten-free baking mix that you prefer, feel free to use that, but know you'll need to adjust the recipe accordingly—adding more or less liquid to get the proper dough or batter consistency and adjusting baking time as needed.

gums

Gums such as xanthan gum and guar gum are main-stays of successful from-scratch gluten-free baking. These gums prevent crumbling and give the stretch and elastic texture that gluten-containing products usually provide in baked goods. These gums are also used commercially as thickeners and stabilizers in salad dressings and pie fillings. Guar gum is less expensive than xanthan gum, but it's also higher in fiber and may have a laxative effect.

We've provided a handful of from-scratch baking recipes in this book using gluten-free flours and gums, but we've also provided recipes using gluten-free baking mixes, which already contain leavening agents, for those who want to save time.

storage and thawing

Gluten-free flours and baked products made with them don't contain preservatives, which means they are more perishable—the flours can become rancid, and gluten-free baked goods dry out more quickly. Proper storage is essential to preserve them as long as possible. Once opened, they should be stored in an airtight container in a dark, dry place. Refrigeration will prolong their shelf life, but bring them to room temperature before using.

Once baked goods are cooled thoroughly, wrap them tightly in plastic wrap, and place them in an airtight container or zip-top plastic freezer bag, removing as much air as possible. Store them in the freezer until ready to use. Breads may be stored at room temperature for a day after baking, and then stored in the freezer until ready to use. They are easiest to use when they have been sliced and each slice has been separated by wax or parchment paper prior to freezing. Most frozen gluten-free baked goods are best when thawed at room temperature because microwaving can make them tough. Toasting is a great way to reheat baked goods and slices of bread.

measuring

Measuring flour and baking mixes is of the utmost importance in light baking because using even a tablespoon or a quarter of an ounce more or less than what we call for in our recipes could result in less-than-favorable results. The most accurate way to measure is by weight, which is why we've given both the ounce weight and approximate cup measures for those who don't have a kitchen scale. Weighing is more accurate and ensures the same great results we produce in our Test Kitchens. If you're using measuring cups, be sure to use dry measuring cups without spouts, and stir the flour or baking mix before spooning it out. (A) Lightly spoon the flour into the measuring cup without compacting it, (B) and then level off the excess with the flat edge of a knife.

If you measure flour or baking mix in other ways (scooping it out of the canister, for example), you may end up with more than intended in the recipe.

gluten-free grains, flours & starches

The products listed on these pages offer some alternatives to gluten-containing ingredients and flours that are helpful to have on hand when baking gluten free.

Cornstarch
Cornstarch is ground from the endosperm of corn kernels. This flavorless powder is used as a binder or thickening agent in puddings, pie fillings, sauces, soups, and stews, and it's added in baked goods to make them lighter in texture.

Arrowroot
Arrowroot is a fine, white powder that resembles cornstarch and is used as a thickener. It is flavorless and sets to an almost clear gel, which makes it ideal for clear sauces. It can replace cornstarch, but leftovers will need to be rethickened.

Xanthan Gum
Gums are a common ingredient in gluten-free baking. They are added to enable rising, reduce crumbling, and give the elastic texture that gluten usually provides. Food manufacturers also use gums as thickeners in salad dressings and pie fillings.

Sorghum Flour
Sorghum flour has a light color and bland flavor that make it a versatile option in gluten-free baking. Since it is milled from the whole grain, it's also higher in fiber and protein than rice flours.

Cornmeal
Cornmeal is made from coarsely grinding whole dried corn, leaving behind the nutrient-packed germ. It is available in white, yellow, and blue, depending on the color of the corn.

White Rice Flour
The bland taste of this flour doesn't alter the flavor of dishes. It comes in a range of textures (from regular to fine) that affect consistency; coarser grinds can create grittiness in baked goods.

Brown Rice Flour
This flour is milled from brown rice, which still contains the bran, giving it a heavier texture, but also making it more nutritious than white rice flour.

Teff

Teff is a very tiny cereal grain native to Africa that's rich in protein, calcium, iron, and potassium. It has a sweet, nutty flavor and can be served alone as a hot cereal or mixed into a variety of baked goods.

Tapioca Flour

This flour (made from the root starch of the cassava plant) produces a clear gel, making it ideal as a thickener in puddings, fruit fillings, soups, and glazes. It also adds chewiness and stretch to gluten-free baked goods.

Hemp Flour

Flour made from hemp seeds is dark in color and imparts a nutty flavor, so it should be used in darker-colored, more strongly flavored baked goods. It is high in fiber and protein, so it is an excellent source of energy.

Garbanzo and Fava Bean Flour

This flour is a protein- and fiber-rich blend of garbanzo beans (chickpeas) and fava beans, which lend an earthy flavor to baked goods. It provides a great texture for a variety of gluten-free baked goods, such as cookies and breads.

Garbanzo Bean Flour

This flour is made by grinding garbanzo beans (also called chickpeas) into a fine protein-rich flour. Use it blended with other flours for all kinds of baking, including cakes, breads, and pizza dough.

Hazelnut Flour

Also referred to as hazelnut meal, this flour is made by grinding hazelnuts. It adds a sweet, nutty flavor to a variety of baked goods. It's also rich in protein and fiber.

Coconut Flour

This high-fiber, protein-rich flour is an excellent gluten-free flour. It gives baked goods a mild sweetness and rich texture. It requires more liquid than other flours, so use it in recipes specifically designed for it.

Almond Flour

Also called almond meal, almond flour is made by grinding raw blanched almonds into a fine powder. Combine it with other gluten-free flours to add a hint of nuttiness plus healthy fats, fiber, and protein.

shopping tips

Successfully avoiding gluten requires you to be a supermarket sleuth with a keen eye for gluten-containing products and ingredients. Here are our tips to get you started.

Always read labels.

For those following a gluten-free diet, reading and decoding labels is vital to successful shopping. The key is knowing what to look for in the sometimes lengthy list of ingredients that may include unfamiliar words. For the ingredients other than wheat and the gluten-containing grains (listed on page 15) that are foreign to you, various websites (see page 11) have lists of ingredients that are safe and forbidden. You may want to print out these lists and take them with you when shopping.

Check labels every time.

Even if the product doesn't say "new" on its package, or if it's a brand that's traditionally safe and that you use often without any problem, you still need to always check ingredient lists for changes. Food manufacturers often tweak their products, ingredients change, and a product that was gluten free and safe may not be so in the newly revamped version.

Shop the perimeter and gluten-free foods aisle.

The perimeter of the grocery store is usually gluten free and should be your main shopping area since it contains fruits, vegetables, fish and shellfish, plain meats and poultry, milk, and eggs. Many grocery stores now have sections devoted entirely to gluten-free foods or shelf tags that point out gluten-free foods, which are extremely helpful when navigating the predominantly gluten-filled aisles.

"Wheat free" doesn't mean gluten free.

Since gluten is also found in rye and barley, a product labeled as wheat free could still contain gluten.

If a label isn't clear, contact the manufacturer.

When a label just isn't clear to you, check the manufacturer's website or contact the manufacturer directly. The customer service center should be able to address your concerns. If they're unsure or can't provide a concrete answer, don't buy the product.

Gluten-Free Pantry and Shopping List

Breads:
__Gluten-free bread, bagels,
  pizza crusts, sandwich buns,
  and rolls
__Gluten-free waffles
__Gluten-free corn tortillas

Cereals:
__Gluten-free cold cereals
  and hot cereals
__Gluten-free cereal bars
__Cornmeal or plain grits

Pasta:
__Corn, bean, potato, quinoa,
  rice, and soy pastas

Rice:
__White, wild, and brown (plain)

Baking Essentials:
__Cornstarch
__Cornmeal
__Gluten-free all-purpose flour
  (a blend of flours)
__Gluten-free baking mixes
  (such as breads, cakes,
  cookies, and brownies)
__Gluten-free pancake/waffle
  mix
__Baking powder
__Baking soda
__Vanilla extract
__Xanthan gum or guar gum

Legumes:
__Dried beans
__Canned beans

Grains:
__Amaranth
__Buckwheat
__Flaxseed
__Millet
__Quinoa

Spices:
__Assorted spices
__Gluten-free seasoning
  packets

Condiments and Sauces:
__Ketchup
__Mustard (plain)
__Relish
__Gluten-free sauce packets
__Tomato sauce
__Mayonnaise
__Gluten-free soy sauce

Miscellaneous:
__Honey, molasses, sugar,
  agave nectar, and stevia
__Jams and jellies
__Gelatin
__Vinegar

Nuts:
__Plain nuts
__Almond, cashew, sunflower
  seeds, and peanut butter

Meat, Fish, and Poultry:
__Fresh or frozen (plain and not
  injected with broth)
__Gluten-free deli meats

Meatless Sources of Protein:
__Tofu (plain)

Dairy:
__Milk
__Plain yogurt
__Cheese (not processed
  cheese)
__Plain cream cheese
__Plain cottage cheese
__Eggs and egg substitute

Fruits:
__Fresh or frozen
__Canned (in syrup or water)

Vegetables:
__Fresh or frozen
__Canned (in water)

Fats and Oils:
__Butter or buttery spread
__Vegetable, olive, and canola
  oils
__Gluten-free salad dressings

Snacks:
__Plain popcorn
__Plain potato and corn chips
__Gluten-free snacks and bars
__Gluten-free crackers

decoding food labels

Reading food labels is a must when living gluten free. Sometimes, the distinctions between gluten-free and gluten-containing foods aren't always obvious until you read the label. Food companies manufacture their products differently, and the ingredients often vary from brand to brand. So it's vital to learn the names of ingredients that could cause concern if you see them on food labels. With practice, patience, and time, label reading will become second nature.

Barley: Barley, a gluten-containing grain, appears on labels as malt, malt extract, malt flavoring, malt syrup, barley malt flavoring, and barley malt syrup. All of these terms indicate the presence of gluten, and the item should be avoided.

Caramel color: This ingredient, when manufactured in North America, is produced from corn and is gluten free.

Hydrolyzed vegetable protein (HVP): This term is not used on a label. Instead, the label must specify the vegetable or grain, such as "hydrolyzed wheat protein," which is not gluten free, or "hydrolyzed soy protein," which is gluten free.

Maltodextrin: This ingredient is made from corn, potato, or rice and should not be confused with the barley-containing ingredients known as malt or malt flavoring. If wheat was used, the label would have to say "wheat maltodextrin" or "maltodextrin (wheat)." The term "dextrin" is rarely used on food labels.

Wheat starch: The starch is used as a binder and thickening agent in foods such as gravies, sauce packets, and seasoning blends. If it is used as an ingredient, the label must say "wheat."

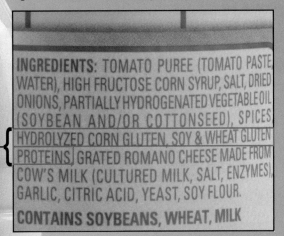

INGREDIENTS: TOMATO PUREE (TOMATO PASTE, WATER), HIGH FRUCTOSE CORN SYRUP, SALT, DRIED ONIONS, PARTIALLY HYDROGENATED VEGETABLE OIL (SOYBEAN AND/OR COTTONSEED), SPICES, HYDROLYZED CORN GLUTEN, SOY & WHEAT GLUTEN PROTEINS, GRATED ROMANO CHEESE MADE FROM COW'S MILK (CULTURED MILK, SALT, ENZYMES), GARLIC, CITRIC ACID, YEAST, SOY FLOUR.

CONTAINS SOYBEANS, WHEAT, MILK

{Check for **Gluten**}

kitchen safety tips

When you or a family member eats gluten free, a safe kitchen is a must. A completely gluten-free kitchen certainly makes shopping and meal planning and preparation easier, and you don't have to worry about cross-contamination issues, but it's not always practical for families whose members are not all required to eat gluten free. If you do have a kitchen that stocks foods containing gluten, you'll be fine; just follow these tips to keep everyone safe.

Wash your hands frequently.

Washing your hands will help prevent cross-contamination of both food and utensils.

Thoroughly clean dishes, counters, and cooking surfaces.

Nonstick pans are easier to clean with little to no food residue left behind. Avoid porous cutting boards, such as wood and bamboo, which are hard to clean and have nooks and crannies where gluten can adhere. Single-use paper towels are best for cleaning up any spills or crumbs and drying hands because fabric dish towels can hold onto gluten-containing crumbs.

Clean kitchen drawers often.

Clean drawers often, especially silverware drawers because they are susceptible to crumbs. You may want to purchase a separate set of cooking and baking tools—perhaps in a different color or brand—to use exclusively for gluten-free meals. Store them in a separate drawer or container so they don't get confused with regular utensils.

Buy two.

Buy separate containers of popular items like peanut butter and jams, and label one container as gluten free to avoid confusion. You wouldn't want someone making a peanut butter and jelly sandwich to stick the wheat crumb–coated knife back in the peanut butter or jelly, making the rest of the jar unsafe for a gluten-free family member. To help avoid this, buy squeeze bottles of condiments when possible to help keep contaminated utensils from coming in contact with the condiment.

Store gluten-free foods separately.

Store foods separately, and clearly label them gluten free. You can color-code the packages and containers with stickers or designate a pantry shelf or area in the refrigerator for only gluten-free items.

Invest in extra appliances.

Invest in an extra colander, sifter, toaster, toaster oven, and other kitchen appliances and utensils that can be difficult to clean. Label them for gluten-free use only.

Prepare gluten-free meals first.

If you're making two meals—one containing gluten and one without—it's best to prepare the gluten-free version first to prevent contamination of work surfaces, cutting boards, and cooking utensils.

Do one thing at a time.

Don't prepare gluten-free meals at the same time you are preparing gluten-containing meals; it's too easy to get confused, and you are more likely to cross-contaminate. Focus on one thing at a time.

Don't reuse.

Do not reuse cooking water if you previously used it for an item containing gluten, such as pasta, or fry regular and gluten-free foods in the same oil.

Beef Stew, page 244

how to use this book

Since following a gluten-free lifestyle can be complicated, our goal when creating The Cooking Light Gluten-Free Cookbook *was to keep things as simple and straight-forward as possible, while providing you with a variety of delicious recipes for every meal.*

In this book, you'll find:
- More than 150 delicious gluten-free recipes.
- Complete nutritional analysis for each recipe so that you can be assured that your meals are gluten free *and* healthy.
- Cooking tips to provide you with extra information about preparing a recipe.
- Comments from individuals following a gluten-free diet who tested and tasted some of these recipes in their own homes.

You'll also notice this phrase next to the names of recipes throughout the book: {Check for **Gluten**}

The recipes that are tagged with this icon contain ingredients that could potentially contain gluten. The ingredients are highlighted in red so you can easily identify them on every page. While label reading is important for all products to ensure the ones you're buying are safe, these products should be rigorously checked at the grocery store to ensure they do not contain gluten.

We've also identified appropriate recipes with this icon: Dairy **free**

Since many people following a gluten-free diet may also follow a dairy-free diet, we've identified those recipes that fit the guidelines.

Appetizers
&Snacks

Roasted Garlic, Poblano, and Red Pepper Guacamole with Homemade Tortilla Chips ☑ Dairy **free**
{Check for **Gluten**}

When storing this guacamole, press plastic wrap against its surface to keep it from turning brown. You can use it to liven up a turkey sandwich or as a condiment in a vegetable wrap.

Guacamole:
- 6 garlic cloves, unpeeled
- 1 red bell pepper
- 1 poblano chile
- ¼ cup finely chopped green onions
- 2 tablespoons chopped fresh cilantro
- 2 teaspoons fresh lime juice
- ¼ teaspoon kosher salt
- 1 ripe peeled avocado, coarsely mashed

Chips:
- 6 (6-inch) corn tortillas, each cut into 8 wedges
- 2 teaspoons fresh lime juice
- ¼ teaspoon kosher salt
- Cooking spray

1. Preheat oven to 450°.

2. To prepare guacamole, wrap garlic cloves in foil; bake at 450° for 15 minutes or until soft. Let cool slightly; remove skins and discard. Place garlic in a medium bowl; mash with a fork.

3. Preheat broiler.

4. Cut bell pepper and poblano in half lengthwise; discard seeds and membranes. Place pepper halves, skin sides up, on a foil-lined baking sheet; flatten with hand. Broil 15 minutes or until blackened, turning frequently. Place in a zip-top plastic bag; seal. Let stand 10 minutes. Peel and finely chop. Add peppers, onions, and next 4 ingredients to mashed garlic; stir well.

5. Reduce oven temperature to 425°.

6. To prepare chips, combine tortilla wedges, 2 teaspoons juice, and ¼ teaspoon salt in a large bowl, tossing to coat. Arrange tortillas in a single layer on a baking sheet coated with cooking spray. Bake at 425° for 10 minutes or until crisp and lightly browned, turning once. Cool 5 minutes. Serve with guacamole.

Yield: 8 servings (serving size: 2½ tablespoons guacamole and 6 chips).

CALORIES 87; FAT 3.7g (sat 1g, mono 1.9g, poly 0.8g); PROTEIN 2.1g; CARB 13.2g; FIBER 3.1g; CHOL 0mg; IRON 0.4mg; SODIUM 151mg; CALC 40mg

Kalamata-Garbanzo Hummus

Tangy Greek yogurt and salty olives give this hummus a Mediterranean kick. Serve with gluten-free rice chips. Opa!

1 large garlic clove
½ cup plain 2% reduced-fat Greek yogurt
2 tablespoons fat-free milk
1 tablespoon cider vinegar
1 tablespoon extra-virgin olive oil
½ teaspoon dried oregano
8 pitted kalamata olives
1 (15½-ounce) can chickpeas (garbanzo beans), rinsed and drained
Chopped kalamata olives (optional)

1. Drop garlic through food chute with food processor on; process until minced. Add yogurt and next 6 ingredients; pulse 10 to 12 times or until desired consistency. Garnish with chopped olives, if desired. **Yield: 7 servings (serving size: ¼ cup).**

CALORIES 77; FAT 4g (sat 0.7g, mono 2.6g, poly 0.5g); PROTEIN 3.5g; CARB 7.1g; FIBER 1.4g; CHOL 1mg; IRON 0.4mg; SODIUM 132mg; CALC 33mg

My family really enjoyed this hummus. It was easy to make and was great with rice chips.

—Connie Hendon

Roasted Sweet Onion Dip

Serve this dip with gluten-free rice crackers or mixed fresh vegetables. Making the recipe a day ahead allows the flavors to meld.

2 large Vidalia or other sweet onions, peeled and quartered
1 tablespoon olive oil
1 teaspoon salt, divided
1 whole garlic head
⅓ cup reduced-fat sour cream
¼ cup chopped fresh parsley
1 tablespoon fresh lemon juice

1. Preheat oven to 425°.
2. Place onion in a large bowl; drizzle with oil. Sprinkle with ½ teaspoon salt; toss to coat. Remove white papery skin from garlic head (do not peel or separate cloves). Wrap in foil. Place onion and foil-wrapped garlic on a baking sheet. Bake at 425° for 1 hour; cool 10 minutes. Chop onion. Separate garlic cloves; squeeze to extract garlic pulp. Discard skins.
3. Combine onion, garlic, remaining ½ teaspoon salt, sour cream, parsley, and lemon juice in a large bowl. Cover and chill 1 hour. **Yield: 8 servings (serving size: ¼ cup).**

CALORIES 66; FAT 2.5g (sat 0.8g, mono 1.3g, poly 0.2g); PROTEIN 1.7g; CARB 10.3g; FIBER 1.5g; CHOL 3mg; IRON 0.4mg; SODIUM 308mg; CALC 42mg

Cooking Tip

Freshly squeezed lemon juice is ideal. Those lemon-shaped plastic bottles do contain real juice, but after it's reconstituted and mixed with preservatives, the taste is notably off, not fresh, a bit harsh and thin. It lasts for months but doesn't really add that divine fresh-lemon essence.

Citrus, Fennel, and Rosemary Olives

☑ Dairy **free**

22 ounces (about 4 cups) assorted olives (such as niçoise, arbequina, kalamata, and picholine)
2 cups extra-virgin olive oil
1 cup finely chopped fennel bulb
1 tablespoon chopped fresh flat-leaf parsley
1½ teaspoons chopped fresh rosemary
1 teaspoon grated lemon rind
¾ teaspoon crushed red pepper
3 garlic cloves, minced

1. Combine all ingredients in a large bowl; stir well to combine. Cover and refrigerate 48 hours. Serve at room temperature.

Yield: 5 cups (serving size: 2 tablespoons).

CALORIES 45; FAT 4.4g (sat 0.6g, mono 3.3g, poly 0.5g); PROTEIN 0.3g; CARB 1.4g; FIBER 0.2g; CHOL 0mg; IRON 0.1mg; SODIUM 200mg; CALC 6mg

Cooking Tip

A mix of fruity and meaty olives works well in this recipe. They are ideal for cocktail platters, antipasto, snacking, or as a gift when placed in a decorative jar. You can refrigerate the olives for up to a month.

Tabbouleh-Style Rice Cucumber Rounds

1 cup cooked brown rice
6 tablespoons (1½ ounces) finely
   grated Asiago cheese
¼ cup finely chopped fresh
   flat-leaf parsley
¼ cup finely chopped bottled
   roasted red bell peppers
1 tablespoon chopped fresh
   oregano
3 tablespoons drained capers
2 teaspoons grated lemon rind
1 tablespoon fresh lemon juice
2 tablespoons extra-virgin
   olive oil
¼ teaspoon salt
⅛ teaspoon crushed red pepper
2 garlic cloves, minced
32 (¼-inch-thick) English
   cucumber slices (about
   1 cucumber)

1. Combine first 12 ingredients; toss gently. Spoon 1 rounded tablespoon rice mixture onto each cucumber slice. **Yield: 8 servings (serving size: 4 cucumber rounds).**

CALORIES 89; FAT 5.5g (sat 1.5g, mono 3.3g, poly 0.5g); PROTEIN 2.2g; CARB 7.9g; FIBER 1g; CHOL 5mg; IRON 0.4mg; SODIUM 229mg; CALC 54mg

Cooking Tip

A handheld grater is an ideal kitchen tool when you need to create finely grated bits that distribute flavor throughout a dish. Use it to grate the rind from fresh citrus or hard cheese, such as the well-aged Asiago and lemon we used in this recipe.

Roasted Vegetable Salsa with Grilled Polenta Cakes

☑ Dairy **free**

The salsa for this recipe makes enough to serve over chicken for another meal or with crackers for a snack. Store extra salsa in the refrigerator for up to 3 days.

4½ cups (1-inch) cubed peeled eggplant (about 1 medium)
2 cups (1-inch) cubed red bell pepper (about 1 medium)
1½ cups (1-inch) pieces onion (about 1 medium)
1 tablespoon olive oil
½ teaspoon salt
½ teaspoon black pepper
1 whole garlic head
2 cups (1-inch) pieces seeded tomato (about 2 medium)
1½ teaspoons grated lemon rind
2 tablespoons fresh lemon juice
½ cup coarsely chopped fresh basil
¼ teaspoon dark sesame oil
1 (17-ounce) tube refrigerated polenta, cut into ½-inch slices
Cooking spray

1. Preheat oven to 425°.

2. Place eggplant, bell pepper, and onion in a single layer on a large jelly-roll pan. Drizzle vegetables with oil; sprinkle with salt and pepper.

3. Remove white papery skin from garlic head (do not peel or separate the cloves). Cut off pointed end of garlic head ¼ inch from top. Wrap garlic in foil, and place on pan. Bake at 425° for 30 minutes. (Do not stir vegetables.)

4. Stir tomato into vegetables, and bake an additional 10 minutes or until vegetables are beginning to brown. Cool in pan on a wire rack 10 minutes.

5. Unwrap garlic. Separate cloves; squeeze to extract pulp into a food processor. Discard skins. Add roasted vegetables, lemon rind, and next 3 ingredients to garlic pulp; pulse 12 times or until chunky, scraping sides of bowl once. Set aside.

6. While vegetables bake, heat a cast-iron grill pan over high heat 4 minutes. While pan heats, pat polenta slices dry with paper towels; coat both sides with cooking spray. Coat pan with cooking spray. Add polenta slices, in batches, to pan; cook 5 minutes on each side or until thoroughly heated and scored with grill marks. Remove from pan; keep warm.

7. Spoon 1½ tablespoons salsa over each polenta cake, reserving remaining salsa for another use. Serve warm. **Yield: 11 servings (serving size: 1 topped polenta cake).**

CALORIES 73; FAT 1.6g (sat 0.2g, mono 1g, poly 0.3g); PROTEIN 2g; CARB 13g; FIBER 3.1g; CHOL 0mg; IRON 0.7mg; SODIUM 187mg; CALC 20mg

Bruschetta with Warm Tomatoes

Use any variety of small summer tomatoes you find at the market; for a gorgeous look, mix tomato colors and shapes, such as yellow and orange pear tomatoes paired with red grape tomatoes.

2½ cups grape, pear, or cherry tomatoes
3 tablespoons thinly sliced fresh basil
2 tablespoons finely chopped shallots
2 teaspoons olive oil
¼ teaspoon sea salt
¼ teaspoon balsamic vinegar
⅛ teaspoon freshly ground black pepper
1 garlic clove, minced
Cooking spray
4 (1-ounce) slices gluten-free French bread
1 garlic clove, halved

1. Combine first 8 ingredients, and let stand 1 hour.
2. Heat a medium nonstick skillet over medium heat. Coat pan with cooking spray. Add tomato mixture, and cook 10 minutes or until thoroughly heated, stirring occasionally. Remove from heat.
3. Heat a grill pan over medium-high heat. Coat pan with cooking spray. Add bread; cook 2 minutes on each side or until toasted. Rub 1 side of each toast slice with the cut sides of garlic clove halves. Serve tomato mixture over toast. **Yield: 4 servings (serving size: 1 toast slice and about ⅓ cup tomato mixture).**

CALORIES 129; FAT 5.5g (sat 0.3g, mono 2.2g, poly 0.5g); PROTEIN 2.8g; CARB 18.5g; FIBER 1.2g; CHOL 26mg; IRON 0.9mg; SODIUM 293mg; CALC 56mg

Cooking Tip

Heating the tomatoes intensifies their sweetness while preserving their bright, fresh flavor.

Smoked Salmon Crostini

You can prepare the salmon topping earlier in the day and keep it refrigerated until ready to assemble. These appetizers look great assembled like canapés. Serve these immediately after toasting and assembling since gluten-free bread can toughen quickly if left out after heating or toasting.

½ cup chopped fennel bulb
¼ cup chopped green onions
1 tablespoon extra-virgin olive oil
2 teaspoons chopped fresh dill
1 teaspoon grated lemon rind
1½ tablespoons fresh lemon juice
1 teaspoon freshly ground black pepper
¾ pound cold-smoked salmon, cut into thin strips
48 (½-inch-thick) slices gluten-free French bread baguette (about 1½ pounds), toasted
½ cup light garlic-and-herbs spreadable cheese
Dill sprigs (optional)

1. Combine first 8 ingredients; cover and chill at least 1 hour. Spread each toast slice with ½ teaspoon cheese; top each with 1 tablespoon salmon mixture. Garnish with dill sprigs, if desired.
Yield: 24 servings (serving size: 2 crostini).

CALORIES 108; FAT 4.7g (sat 0.7g, mono 1.2g, poly 0.4g); PROTEIN 4.7g; CARB 14.1g; FIBER 0.1g; CHOL 32mg; IRON 0.7mg; SODIUM 274mg; CALC 44mg

Beef Teriyaki Crisps with Wasabi Mayonnaise

{Check for **Gluten**}

Prepare the mayonnaise mixture and cook the steak up to a day in advance. There's no need to reheat it; just slice the steak about an hour ahead, and leave at room temperature.

¼ cup fresh orange juice
¼ cup lower-sodium soy sauce
2 tablespoons mirin (sweet rice wine)
2 tablespoons honey
2 teaspoons grated peeled fresh ginger
½ pound flank steak, trimmed
Cooking spray
½ cup reduced-fat mayonnaise
2 teaspoons wasabi paste
2 teaspoons rice vinegar
24 baked gluten-free rice crackers
Fresh chive pieces (optional)

1. Combine first 6 ingredients in a large zip-top plastic bag; seal. Marinate in refrigerator 24 hours, turning occasionally.

2. Remove steak from bag, and discard marinade. Heat a grill pan over medium-high heat. Coat pan with cooking spray. Add steak to pan; grill 6 minutes on each side or until desired degree of doneness. Remove steak from pan; let stand 10 minutes. Cut steak diagonally across grain into thin slices; cut slices into 2-inch pieces.

3. Combine mayonnaise, wasabi paste, and vinegar, stirring well. Spoon ¾ teaspoon mayonnaise mixture onto each cracker. Divide steak evenly among crackers; top each with ¼ teaspoon mayonnaise mixture. Garnish with chives, if desired. **Yield: 12 servings (serving size: 2 topped crisps).**

CALORIES 71; FAT 2.6g (sat 0.5g, mono 0.4g, poly 0.7g); PROTEIN 4.2g; CARB 7.1g; FIBER 0g; CHOL 7mg; IRON 0.3mg; SODIUM 166mg; CALC 3mg

Cooking Tip

Mirin is a kind of Japanese rice wine similar to sake but with a lower alcohol content. It's a clear, gold liquid that adds a mild sweetness to dishes and a slight sheen to meats, fish, and shellfish.

Tempura Green Beans with Mild Cayenne Sour Cream

Batters like this one that use carbonated beverages such as club soda produce gas bubbles that discourage oil absorption, yielding a lighter fried food.

4	cups canola oil
4.4	ounces gluten-free all-purpose flour (about 1 cup; such as Bob's Red Mill)
5	ounces white rice flour (about 1 cup; such as Bob's Red Mill)
2	teaspoons paprika
1	teaspoon baking soda
½	teaspoon black pepper
1¼	cups club soda, chilled
8	ounces green beans, trimmed
½	teaspoon kosher salt
	Mild Cayenne Sour Cream

1. Preheat oven to 200°.

2. Clip a candy thermometer onto the side of a 4-quart Dutch oven; add oil to pan. Heat oil to 385°.

3. While oil heats, weigh or lightly spoon flours into dry measuring cups; level with a knife. Combine flours, paprika, baking soda, and black pepper in a medium bowl. Gradually add club soda, stirring with a whisk until smooth.

4. Dip beans, 1 at a time, in batter, coating completely. Add to hot oil in a single layer. (Do not crowd pan.) Fry, in batches, 1 minute or until golden, turning once. (Maintain temperature of oil at 375°.) Drain beans on a paper towel–lined jelly-roll pan. Place pan in oven, and keep warm at 200° until ready to serve. Sprinkle beans evenly with salt just before serving. Serve with Mild Cayenne Sour Cream. **Yield: 8 servings (serving size: ⅛ of beans and 1 tablespoon sauce).**

CALORIES 240; FAT 15.9g (sat 2.1g, mono 8.9g, poly 4g); PROTEIN 3.4g; CARB 22.3g; FIBER 2.7g; CHOL 5mg; IRON 0.6mg; SODIUM 337mg; CALC 25mg

Mild Cayenne Sour Cream:

Combine ½ cup light sour cream, 1 tablespoon water, ½ teaspoon Dijon mustard, ¼ teaspoon salt, and a dash of ground red pepper in a small bowl. Stir in 2 teaspoons prepared horseradish, if desired. **Yield: ½ cup (serving size: 1 tablespoon).**

CALORIES 20; FAT 1.3g (sat 1g, mono 0g, poly 0g); PROTEIN 1g; CARB 1.1g; FIBER 0g; CHOL 5mg; IRON 0mg; SODIUM 93mg; CALC 0mg

Diner-Style Onion Rings

 Dairy **free**

4 cups canola oil

4.4 ounces gluten-free all-purpose flour (about 1 cup; such as Bob's Red Mill)

5 ounces white rice flour (about 1 cup; such as Bob's Red Mill)

1 tablespoon chili powder

1 teaspoon baking soda

1¼ cups club soda, chilled

1 medium onion, cut into ½-inch-thick slices and separated into rings (8 ounces)

¼ teaspoon salt

¼ teaspoon garlic powder

¼ teaspoon black pepper

½ cup ketchup (optional)

1. Preheat oven to 200°.

2. Clip a candy thermometer onto the side of a 4-quart Dutch oven; add oil to pan. Heat oil to 385°.

3. While oil heats, weigh or lightly spoon flours into dry measuring cups; level with a knife. Combine flours, chili powder, and baking soda in a medium bowl. Gradually add club soda, stirring with a whisk until smooth.

4. Dip onion rings, 1 at a time, in batter, coating completely. Add to hot oil. (Do not crowd pan.) Fry 1 minute on each side or until golden, maintaining temperature of oil at 375°. Drain onion rings on a paper towel–lined jelly-roll pan. Place pan in oven and keep warm at 200° until ready to serve. Combine salt, garlic powder, and black pepper. Sprinkle onion rings evenly with salt mixture just before serving. Serve with ketchup, if desired. **Yield: 6 servings (serving size: about 5 onion rings).**

CALORIES 234; FAT 19g (sat 1.4g, mono 11.9g, poly 5.3g); PROTEIN 1.7g; CARB 15.4g; FIBER 1.7g; CHOL 0mg; IRON 0.4mg; SODIUM 177mg; CALC 17mg

Cooking Tip

You'll have some of the batter left over, but don't decrease the amount you use. You need the full amount so the onion rings can be immersed in batter and get fully coated.

Quick Calamari with Garlic Mayo

Mayo:
- ¼ cup light mayonnaise
- 1 garlic clove, minced
- 1 teaspoon lemon juice
- 1 teaspoon chopped fresh parsley

Calamari:
- 1 pound squid tubes and tentacles
- ¼ cup yellow cornmeal (such as Bob's Red Mill)
- 2 tablespoons cornstarch
- 2 teaspoons paprika
- ¼ teaspoon salt
- ½ cup vegetable oil, divided
- 1 lemon, cut into 6 wedges

1. To prepare mayo, combine first 4 ingredients in a small bowl. Cover and chill.

2. To prepare calamari, cut squid tubes into ½-inch rings. Leave tentacles intact. Rinse and pat dry.

3. Combine cornmeal and next 3 ingredients in a large heavy-duty zip-top plastic bag; add half of squid. Seal bag; shake to coat.

4. Heat ¼ cup oil in a large skillet over high heat. Add squid coated with cornmeal mixture to hot oil; cook 2 minutes, turning frequently, or until squid begins to curl around edges. (Do not overcook.) Remove squid from pan; drain on paper towels. Repeat procedure with remaining squid, cornmeal mixture, and ¼ cup oil. Serve immediately with garlic mayo and lemon wedges. **Yield: 6 servings (serving size: ½ cup calamari, 2 teaspoons mayo, and 1 lemon wedge).**

CALORIES 238; FAT 16.1g (sat 2g, mono 5.8g, poly 6.6g); PROTEIN 12.4g; CARB 11g; FIBER 0.5g; CHOL 180mg; IRON 0.9mg; SODIUM 191mg; CALC 28mg

Cooking Tip

Calamari has a reputation for being rubbery, but it only becomes tough if it's overcooked. For pan-frying, use a skillet or sauté pan—a wide pan with sloped or straight sides. Choose a heavy-bottomed pan for evenly distributed heat with no hot spots. Also, the key when pan-frying is to make sure your oil is hot and then cook the food quickly.

Mini Crab Cake Quiches with Chili-Lime Sauce

{Check for **Gluten**}

Sauce:
- ½ cup reduced-fat mayonnaise
- 1½ teaspoons grated lime rind
- 2 teaspoons fresh lime juice
- 1 small garlic clove, pressed
- ⅛ teaspoon ground red pepper

Quiches:
- ¼ cup gluten-free panko-style breadcrumbs (such as Kinnikinnick)
- 2 teaspoons Old Bay seasoning
- 1 teaspoon baking powder
- 1 teaspoon dry mustard
- ⅛ teaspoon freshly ground black pepper
- 3 tablespoons reduced-fat mayonnaise
- 1 tablespoon fresh lemon juice
- 1 teaspoon Worcestershire sauce
- 3 large eggs
- 1 pound jumbo lump crabmeat, drained and shell pieces removed
- Cooking spray

1. To prepare sauce, combine first 5 ingredients in a small bowl, stirring with a whisk until smooth. Cover and refrigerate.

2. To prepare quiches, preheat oven to 375°.

3. Combine breadcrumbs and next 4 ingredients in a small bowl. Combine mayonnaise and next 3 ingredients in a medium bowl, stirring with a whisk until eggs are beaten. Fold crabmeat into egg mixture; fold in breadcrumb mixture. Lightly spoon crab mixture evenly into 24 miniature muffin cups coated with cooking spray.

4. Bake at 375° for 15 minutes or until set and beginning to brown. Cool in pans 5 minutes before serving. Run a small sharp knife around edges of quiches; remove from muffin cups, and place on a serving platter. Serve with sauce. **Yield: 12 servings (serving size: 2 quiches and 2 teaspoons sauce).**

CALORIES 70; FAT 2.4g (sat 0.4g, mono 0.5g, poly 0.6g); PROTEIN 9.1g; CARB 3.4g; FIBER 0.1g; CHOL 97mg; IRON 10.4mg; SODIUM 445mg; CALC 37mg

Oh my gosh! These were so good!
Neither my husband nor I could tell any difference between this recipe and the other crab cake recipes that I remember from my gluten days. That is the mark of a successful gluten-free recipe!

—Peggy Christoffer

Grilled Shrimp with Romesco Sauce

☑ Dairy **free**

1 cup canned fire-roasted diced tomatoes, drained
¼ cup slivered almonds, toasted
2 tablespoons olive oil
1 tablespoon red wine vinegar
2 teaspoons crushed red pepper
1 teaspoon ground cumin
¾ teaspoon salt
3 garlic cloves, chopped
2 (7½-ounce) jars roasted red bell peppers, drained
1 (1-ounce) slice gluten-free white bread
48 large fresh shrimp (about 3 pounds)
Cooking spray
Chopped fresh parsley (optional)

1. Preheat grill to medium-high heat.

2. Place first 10 ingredients in a food processor, and process until smooth.

3. Place shrimp on grill rack coated with cooking spray. Grill shrimp 3 minutes on each side or until done. Garnish with parsley, if desired, and serve with sauce. **Yield: 12 servings (serving size: 4 shrimp and about 2½ tablespoons sauce).**

CALORIES 170; FAT 5.5g (sat 0.8g, mono 2.6g, poly 1.3g); PROTEIN 23.9g; CARB 4.7g; FIBER 0.7g; CHOL 172mg; IRON 3.1mg; SODIUM 419mg; CALC 72mg

Cooking Tip

To get a head start on this appetizer, you can prepare and refrigerate the no-cook sauce the night before. Store it in an airtight container, and then set it out while you grill your shrimp so it can come to room temperature; or, serve the sauce chilled, if you like.

Coconut Shrimp with Mango Sauce

☑ Dairy **free**
{Check for **Gluten**}

20 large shrimp (about 1¼ pounds)
½ cup gluten-free panko-style breadcrumbs (such as Kinnikinnick)
¾ cup flaked sweetened coconut
1 teaspoon garlic powder
¼ teaspoon salt
2 large egg whites
Mango Sauce

1. Preheat oven to 425°.

2. Peel shrimp, leaving tails intact. Starting at tail end, butterfly each shrimp, cutting to, but not through, backside of shrimp.

3. Combine breadcrumbs and next 3 ingredients in a shallow bowl. Beat egg whites with a whisk until foamy in a separate bowl. Add half of shrimp to egg whites, tossing to coat. Dredge shrimp in coconut mixture, pressing gently to adhere. Place shrimp on a parchment paper–lined baking sheet. Repeat procedure with remaining shrimp, egg whites, and coconut mixture.

4. Bake at 425° for 6 minutes. Using tongs, grasp shrimp by tails and turn over. Bake an additional 6 minutes or until golden brown. Serve shrimp with Mango Sauce. **Yield: 4 servings (serving size: 5 shrimp and 2 tablespoons sauce).**

CALORIES 264; FAT 6g (sat 3.6g, mono 0.6g, poly 1g); PROTEIN 31.7g; CARB 20.6g; FIBER 2.4g; CHOL 216mg; IRON 3.8mg; SODIUM 783mg; CALC 94mg

Mango Sauce:

Place 1¼ cups chopped peeled ripe mango (about 1 large), 1 tablespoon fish sauce, 1½ teaspoons light brown sugar, ½ teaspoon garlic powder, 1½ teaspoons chili garlic sauce, and 1½ teaspoons fresh lime juice in a blender; process 30 seconds or until smooth. Spoon into a small serving bowl. **Yield: ½ cup (serving size: 1 tablespoon).**

CALORIES 21; FAT 0.1g (sat 0g, mono 0g, poly 0g); PROTEIN 0.3g; CARB 5.3g; FIBER 0.5g; CHOL 0mg; IRON 0.1mg; SODIUM 188mg; CALC 4mg

Spiced Pecan-Cherry Crunch Mix

 Dairy **free**

1 large egg white
¼ cup sugar
1½ teaspoons ground cinnamon
¼ teaspoon ground nutmeg
⅛ teaspoon salt
2 cups gluten-free oven-toasted rice cereal (such as Koala)
¾ cup pecan halves, coarsely chopped
⅓ cup dried cherries
2 teaspoons grated orange rind
Cooking spray

1. Preheat oven to 300°.

2. Beat egg white with a mixer at medium speed in a medium bowl until foamy. Combine sugar and next 3 ingredients. Add sugar mixture to beaten egg white, 1 tablespoon at a time, beating until stiff peaks form. Fold in cereal and next 3 ingredients. Spread cereal mixture on a foil-lined baking sheet coated with cooking spray.

3. Bake at 300° for 20 minutes, stirring after 10 minutes. Cool completely in pan on a wire rack. Store in an airtight container.

Yield: 6 servings (serving size: ½ cup).

CALORIES 205; FAT 9.5g (sat 0.8g, mono 5.1g, poly 2.7g); PROTEIN 2.9g; CARB 28.9g; FIBER 3.4g; CHOL 0mg; IRON 1.8mg; SODIUM 103mg; CALC 26mg

Cooking Tip

This is a versatile snack mix, so feel free to substitute another type of nut in place of the pecans (almonds would be delicious), or try dried cranberries or raisins in place of the cherries.

Spicy Almond-Pumpkinseed Snack Mix

☑ Dairy **free**
{Check for **Gluten**}

This snack mix stores well for up to a week in an airtight container.

2 cups gluten-free crispy rice cereal squares (such as Rice Chex)
½ cup salted roasted whole pumpkinseeds
⅓ cup slivered almonds
1 tablespoon canola oil
2 teaspoons chili powder
2 teaspoons Worcestershire sauce
2 teaspoons prepared mustard
½ teaspoon Spanish smoked paprika
¼ teaspoon ground cumin
¼ teaspoon ground red pepper
Cooking spray
¼ teaspoon salt

1. Preheat oven to 300°.

2. Combine first 3 ingredients in a large bowl. Combine oil and next 6 ingredients in a small bowl; drizzle over cereal mixture, tossing well to coat.

3. Line a large jelly-roll pan with foil; coat foil with cooking spray. Spread cereal mixture on prepared pan.

4. Bake at 300° for 10 minutes; stir. Bake an additional 7 minutes or just until mixture begins to brown. Remove from oven; sprinkle with salt, and stir well. Cool in pan on a wire rack. Store in an airtight container. **Yield: 6 servings (serving size: ½ cup).**

CALORIES 118; FAT 6.7g (sat 0.6g, mono 3.7g, poly 1.9g); PROTEIN 3g; CARB 12.5g; FIBER 1g; CHOL 0mg; IRON 3.6mg; SODIUM 272mg; CALC 56mg

Honey-Roasted Nuts and Fruit

Use any variety of mixed nuts or seeds you like in this trail mix. Dried fruit is rich in vitamins and antioxidants, and the nuts add healthy fats and protein, which makes this an excellent on-the-go snack.

Cooking spray
1 teaspoon butter
¼ cup honey
¼ cup slivered almonds
¼ cup chopped hazelnuts
¼ cup chopped pecans
¼ cup sunflower seed kernels
½ teaspoon ground cinnamon
¼ teaspoon salt
¼ teaspoon ground cardamom
Dash of ground cloves
1 cup raisins

1. Line a baking sheet with parchment paper or foil; coat with cooking spray.
2. Heat butter in a large nonstick skillet over medium-high heat. Stir in honey; cook 2 minutes or until mixture bubbles around edges of pan. Add almonds and next 7 ingredients; cook over medium heat 8 minutes or until nuts are golden, stirring frequently. Stir in raisins. Immediately spread onto prepared baking sheet; cool completely. **Yield: 8 servings (serving size: ¼ cup).**

CALORIES 194; FAT 9.4g (sat 1g, mono 5g, poly 2.8g); PROTEIN 3.4g; CARB 27.8g; FIBER 2.2g; CHOL 2mg; IRON 1mg; SODIUM 82mg; CALC 30mg

Cooking Tip

Lining the baking sheet with parchment paper or foil and then coating it with cooking spray prevents the honey-coated nuts and fruit from sticking to the pan. It also makes cleanup a cinch.

Indian-Spiced Roasted Nuts

☑ Dairy **free**

This simple recipe makes a tasty party snack. Use your favorite nuts, and add a bit of heat with a dash of ground red pepper, if you like.

1½ teaspoons brown sugar
1½ teaspoons honey
 1   teaspoon canola oil
 ¾   teaspoon ground cinnamon
 ⅛   teaspoon salt
 ⅛   teaspoon ground cardamom
 ⅛   teaspoon ground cloves
     Dash of freshly ground black
       pepper
 ¼   cup blanched almonds
 ¼   cup cashews
 ¼   cup hazelnuts

1. Preheat oven to 350°.

2. Combine first 8 ingredients in a microwave-safe bowl. Microwave at HIGH 30 seconds; stir until blended. Add nuts to sugar mixture; toss to coat.

3. Spread nuts evenly on a baking sheet lined with parchment paper. Bake at 350° for 15 minutes or until golden brown. Cool.
Yield: 12 servings (serving size: 1 tablespoon).

CALORIES 60; FAT 5g (sat 0.5g, mono 3.3g, poly 0.9g); PROTEIN 1.5g; CARB 3.4g; FIBER 0.8g; CHOL 0mg; IRON 0.5mg; SODIUM 44mg; CALC 14mg

Cooking Tip

Measuring honey can be a mess since the golden-hued liquid likes to stick. Try lightly coating your measuring spoons or cups with cooking spray to prevent sticking.

Chocolate-Almond Pretzels

{Check for **Gluten**}

45 gluten-free pretzel twists (such as Glutino)

⅔ cup semisweet chocolate chips

3 tablespoons sliced almonds, toasted and finely chopped

1. Arrange pretzels in a single layer on a foil-lined baking sheet.

2. Place chocolate chips in a small microwave-safe bowl. Microwave at HIGH 1 minute and 20 seconds or until melted, stirring every 30 seconds. Spoon chocolate into a snack-sized zip-top plastic bag. Snip a tiny hole in 1 corner of bag; drizzle chocolate over pretzels, and sprinkle with almonds.

3. Let stand at room temperature 4 hours or until chocolate is firm. Store in an airtight container. **Yield: 5 servings (serving size: 9 pretzels).**

CALORIES 179; FAT 10.6g (sat 5g, mono 3.3g, poly 0.6g); PROTEIN 1.7g; CARB 22.6g; FIBER 1.7g; CHOL 0mg; IRON 0.8mg; SODIUM 160mg; CALC 16mg

Cooking Tip

Toasting almonds gives them a richer, nuttier taste. Simply spread the almonds on a baking sheet, and bake at 350° for 6 to 8 minutes. Or, place the almonds in a dry skillet, and cook over medium heat, stirring frequently, 1 to 2 minutes or until they're toasted. Be sure to watch them carefully—they can go from toasted to burned very quickly.

Breakfast

Sweet Almond Cream of Buckwheat with Skillet Pears

2 cups fat-free milk
½ cup uncooked cream of buckwheat
2 tablespoons plus 2 teaspoons sugar, divided
1 tablespoon light butter
½ teaspoon vanilla extract
¼ teaspoon almond extract
¼ teaspoon salt
Cooking spray
2 cups chopped ripe pear
¼ cup dried cherries
2 tablespoons water
½ teaspoon ground cinnamon
¼ cup sliced almonds, toasted

1. Bring milk just to a boil in a medium saucepan over medium-high heat. Stir in cream of buckwheat; reduce heat and simmer 10 minutes or until thickened, stirring frequently. Remove buckwheat from heat; stir in 2 tablespoons sugar, butter, and next 3 ingredients.
2. While buckwheat cooks, heat a medium nonstick skillet over medium-high heat. Coat pan with cooking spray. Add pear, remaining 2 teaspoons sugar, cherries, 2 tablespoons water, and cinnamon to pan. Bring to a simmer; cover and cook 4 minutes. Remove from heat.
3. Spoon cereal evenly into 4 bowls. Top evenly with pear mixture and almonds. **Yield: 4 servings (serving size: ½ cup cereal, ½ cup pears, and 1 tablespoon almonds).**

CALORIES 328; FAT 5.4g (sat 1.2g, mono 2.1g, poly 0.8g); PROTEIN 9g; CARB 65.3g; FIBER 8.6g; CHOL 6mg; IRON 1.2mg; SODIUM 224mg; CALC 213mg

Cooking Tip

Buckwheat is a misleading term. It's not wheat but rather a naturally gluten-free seed that yields this delicious, creamy hot breakfast. It's a whole grain, which carries many health benefits such as helping to reduce blood cholesterol levels, and is less starchy and higher in fiber than gluten-free corn or rice.

Hot Quinoa Cereal with Maple Syrup Apples

Once cooked, quinoa flakes are very similar in texture to cream of wheat.

2 cups diced Granny Smith apple
¼ cup water
½ teaspoon ground cinnamon
⅛ teaspoon ground nutmeg
Dash of ground cloves
2 cups water
⅔ cup quinoa flakes
⅛ teaspoon salt
2 tablespoons sugar
3 tablespoons pure maple syrup
2 tablespoons butter
1 teaspoon vanilla extract

1. Combine apple and ¼ cup water in a small skillet; bring to a boil. Stir in cinnamon, nutmeg, and cloves; cover, reduce heat, and simmer 4 minutes or just until crisp-tender. Remove from heat; uncover and let stand.

2. Bring 2 cups water to a boil in a large saucepan over high heat; stir in quinoa flakes and salt. Cook 1½ minutes, stirring frequently. Remove from heat; stir in sugar, and let stand 5 minutes or until slightly thickened.

3. While cereal stands, return apple mixture to medium heat; add syrup, butter, and vanilla, stirring just until butter melts. Serve apple mixture over cereal. **Yield: 4 servings (serving size: about ½ cup cereal and 6 tablespoons apples).**

CALORIES 217; FAT 6.9g (sat 3.7g, mono 1.5g, poly 0.3g); PROTEIN 2.4g; CARB 37.1g; FIBER 2.9g; CHOL 15mg; IRON 1.6mg; SODIUM 117mg; CALC 19mg

Cooking Tip

Pure vanilla extract is made from distilled alcohol and flavor extracted from the vanilla seeds (artificial extract gets its vanilla flavor from artificial vanilla flavoring). The distillation process removes the gluten from the alcohol. This is true of other extracts too, such as almond and banana.

Pear-Almond Muffins

1½ cups chopped peeled ripe
    Bartlett pear (about 2 medium)
  1 tablespoon fresh lemon juice
  2 teaspoons sugar
8.6 ounces gluten-free baking and
    pancake mix (about 2 cups;
    such as Pamela's)
  ¾ cup slivered almonds
  ½ cup sugar
  2 large eggs
  1 teaspoon vanilla extract
  ½ teaspoon almond extract
  Cooking spray

1. Preheat oven to 350°.
2. Combine first 3 ingredients in a microwave-safe bowl. Microwave at HIGH 4 minutes or until pear is very tender. Mash pear with a potato masher until pureed. Cool slightly.
3. While pear puree cools, weigh or lightly spoon baking mix into dry measuring cups; level with a knife. Place almonds in a food processor; process 40 seconds or until finely ground. Combine baking mix, almonds, and ½ cup sugar in a medium bowl; stir with a whisk. Make a well in center of mixture. Combine eggs, extracts, and pear puree, stirring well with a whisk. Add to almond mixture, stirring just until moist. Spoon batter evenly into 12 muffin cups coated with cooking spray.
4. Bake at 350° for 23 minutes or until muffins spring back when touched lightly in center. **Yield: 12 servings (serving size: 1 muffin).**

CALORIES 181; FAT 6g (sat 0.8g, mono 3g, poly 1.5g); PROTEIN 4.6g; CARB 27.6g; FIBER 2.2g; CHOL 38mg; IRON 0.6mg; SODIUM 210mg; CALC 75mg

The recipe was simple and easy to follow, and I had most of the ingredients already in my pantry.

—*Betty Barfield*

Strawberry Muffins

5.4 ounces gluten-free baking and pancake mix (about 1¼ cups; such as Pamela's)
½ cup packed light brown sugar
6 tablespoons fat-free milk
3 tablespoons butter, melted
1 tablespoon vanilla extract
1 large egg
¼ cup diced strawberries
1 teaspoon gluten-free baking and pancake mix (such as Pamela's)
¼ cup sliced strawberries

1. Preheat oven to 375°.

2. Weigh or lightly spoon 1¼ cups baking mix into dry measuring cups; level with a knife. Combine baking mix and brown sugar in a medium bowl; stir with a whisk. Make a well in center of mixture. Combine milk and next 3 ingredients in a bowl, stirring well with a whisk. Add to baking mix mixture; stir just until moist.

3. Place 12 muffin cup liners in muffin cups. Combine diced strawberries and 1 teaspoon baking mix; toss lightly. Spoon half of batter evenly into liners. Top each with 1 teaspoon diced strawberry mixture. Spoon remaining batter evenly over strawberries. Place 1 strawberry slice on top of each muffin.

4. Bake at 375° for 14 minutes or until muffins spring back when touched lightly in center. Cool in pans 5 minutes. Remove from pans; serve warm. **Yield: 12 servings (serving size: 1 muffin).**

CALORIES 126; FAT 4.5g (sat 2.1g, mono 0.9g, poly 0.2g); PROTEIN 2.2g; CARB 18.9g; FIBER 0.6g; CHOL 27mg; IRON 0.3mg; SODIUM 159mg; CALC 54mg

Cooking Tip

We tossed the strawberries with a teaspoon of gluten-free baking mix and added them between two layers of batter to keep them from sinking to the bottom as the muffins bake. The strawberry slices on top are a pretty way to finish them off.

Cinnamon-Raisin Muffins with Streusel Topping

☑ Dairy **free**

Streusel:
- ¼ cup chopped walnuts
- ¼ cup packed light brown sugar
- 2 tablespoons brown rice flour (such as Bob's Red Mill)
- ½ teaspoon ground cinnamon
- 1½ tablespoons canola oil or butter

Muffins:
- Cooking spray
- 3.3 ounces brown rice flour (about ¾ cup; such as Bob's Red Mill)
- 4.1 ounces potato starch (about ¾ cup)
- 2.1 ounces tapioca flour (about ½ cup)
- ¾ cup granulated sugar
- 1 tablespoon baking powder
- 1½ teaspoons xanthan gum
- ½ teaspoon ground cinnamon
- ½ teaspoon salt
- ¾ cup raisins
- ¼ cup chopped toasted walnuts
- ⅓ cup canola oil
- 1 teaspoon vanilla extract
- 2 large eggs
- 1 cup plain soy milk

1. Preheat oven to 400°.

2. To prepare streusel, combine first 5 ingredients in a small bowl with a fork until mixture resembles small peas.

3. To prepare muffins, place 18 paper muffin cup liners in muffin cups. Coat liners with cooking spray; set aside.

4. Weigh or lightly spoon brown rice flour, potato starch, and tapioca flour into dry measuring cups; level with a knife. Combine brown rice flour, potato starch, tapioca flour, granulated sugar, and next 4 ingredients in a large bowl, stirring with a whisk. Stir in raisins and walnuts; make a well in center of mixture. Combine oil, vanilla, and eggs in a medium bowl, stirring with a whisk. Stir in soy milk; add to rice flour mixture, stirring just until moist. Spoon batter evenly into prepared muffin cups. Sprinkle batter evenly with streusel topping.

5. Bake at 400° for 20 minutes or until muffins are lightly browned and spring back when touched lightly in center. Cool in pans 5 minutes on a wire rack. Serve warm. **Yield: 18 servings (serving size: 1 muffin).**

CALORIES 201; FAT 8.5g (sat 0.8g, mono 3.9g, poly 3.2g); PROTEIN 2.3g; CARB 31g; FIBER 1g; CHOL 24mg; IRON 0.6mg; SODIUM 149mg; CALC 57mg

These muffins smelled so good while they were cooking. The first words out of my mouth after the first bite were literally, **"Holy moly! These are amazing!!!"** I haven't had real muffins in several years, so I tried them out on unsuspecting "normal" folks. I took a dozen of them to some friends, and they went nuts over them. No one could tell they were gluten free. They were light and fluffy, flavorful, and exceptionally delicious.

—*Brandi B. Frederick*

Peanut Butter and Banana Pancakes

You can give these pancakes a PB&J flavor profile by spreading them with grape or strawberry jelly. Or just drizzle them with syrup.

5.4 ounces gluten-free baking and pancake mix (about 1¼ cups; such as Pamela's)
 1 cup warm water
 ½ cup creamy peanut butter
 ⅛ teaspoon salt
 1 large egg
 ½ cup chopped banana (about 1 small)

1. Weigh or lightly spoon baking mix into dry measuring cups; level with a knife. Combine baking mix and next 4 ingredients in a medium bowl, stirring well with a whisk. Fold in banana.

2. Heat a large nonstick skillet or griddle over medium heat. Pour ¼ cup batter per pancake onto hot pan. Cook 2 to 3 minutes or until tops are covered with bubbles and edges look cooked. Carefully turn pancakes over; cook 2 to 3 minutes or until bottoms are lightly browned. Repeat procedure with remaining batter. **Yield: 5 servings (serving size: 2 pancakes).**

CALORIES 301; FAT 16.6g (sat 3.4g, mono 7.5g, poly 4.6g); PROTEIN 10.9g; CARB 29.2g; FIBER 3.1g; CHOL 46mg; IRON 1mg; SODIUM 488mg; CALC 94mg

Sour Cream–Blueberry Pancakes

1 cup light sour cream
1 tablespoon sugar
1 teaspoon vanilla extract
2 large eggs
2.15 ounces gluten-free baking and pancake mix (about ½ cup; such as Pamela's)
¼ teaspoon salt
Cooking spray
1 cup blueberries, divided

1. Combine first 4 ingredients in a medium bowl, stirring well with a whisk. Weigh or lightly spoon baking mix into a dry measuring cup; level with a knife. Add baking mix and salt to sour cream mixture, stirring just until moistened.

2. Heat a large nonstick skillet or griddle over medium-high heat. Coat pan with cooking spray. Pour about ¼ cup batter per pancake onto hot pan; cook 1 minute. Sprinkle each pancake with 1 tablespoon blueberries. Cook 1 minute or until edges look cooked. Carefully turn pancakes over; cook 2 minutes or until bottoms are lightly browned. Repeat procedure with remaining batter. Top pancakes evenly with remaining ½ cup blueberries. **Yield: 4 servings (serving size: 2 pancakes and 2 tablespoons blueberries).**

CALORIES 229; FAT 11.6g (sat 5.7g, mono 3.7g, poly 1.3g); PROTEIN 7.7g; CARB 23.1g; FIBER 1.5g; CHOL 139mg; IRON 0.8mg; SODIUM 365mg; CALC 153mg

Cooking Tip

Gluten-free baking mix is the key to quick gluten-free baking. We tested our pancake recipes with a variety of baking mixes and found that each baking mix produced its own results. Some of the mixes were more finely textured, and some were coarser, which affected both the thickness of the batter and the texture. Our advice: Use the brand you prefer. If you're not sure, experiment with a few to find the texture and flavor that appeal to your tastes.

Griddlecakes with Sweet Lemon Butter and Blueberries

You could top these pancakes with strawberries, raspberries, or any combination of your favorite berries.

7.1 ounces gluten-free pancake
    mix (about 1½ cups; such as
    Bob's Red Mill)
1 large egg
1 cup low-fat buttermilk
1 tablespoon canola oil
2 tablespoons grated lemon rind,
    divided
1½ cups blueberries, divided
3 tablespoons powdered sugar
2 tablespoons light butter,
    softened
    Cooking spray

1. Weigh or lightly spoon pancake mix into dry measuring cups; level with a knife. Place pancake mix in a medium bowl. Combine egg, buttermilk, oil, and 1 tablespoon lemon rind, stirring with a whisk; add to pancake mix, stirring until smooth. Fold in ½ cup blueberries; let stand 5 minutes.

2. While batter stands, combine powdered sugar, butter, and remaining 1 tablespoon lemon rind, stirring with a fork.

3. Heat a large nonstick skillet over medium-high heat. Coat pan with cooking spray. Pour about ¼ cup batter per pancake onto hot pan. Cook 1 minute or until tops are covered with bubbles and edges look cooked. Carefully turn pancakes over; cook 1 minute or until bottoms are lightly browned. Repeat procedure with remaining batter.

4. Spread pancakes evenly with butter mixture and top evenly with remaining 1 cup blueberries. **Yield: 4 servings (serving size: 2 pancakes, about 1 tablespoon lemon butter, and ¼ cup blueberries).**

CALORIES 391; FAT 9.3g (sat 3.4g, mono 4.1g, poly 1.4g); PROTEIN 7.3g; CARB 71.4g; FIBER 1.7g; CHOL 55mg; IRON 0.5mg; SODIUM 549mg; CALC 238mg

Toaster Waffles with Lemon-Ginger Berry Sauce and Sweet Yogurt

Dress up frozen waffles with a delicious fruit sauce and easy yogurt topping.

1 (12-ounce) carton plain 2% reduced-fat Greek yogurt
6 tablespoons sugar, divided
1 tablespoon vanilla extract, divided
4 cups frozen unsweetened mixed berries
¼ cup water
2 teaspoons cornstarch
2 teaspoons grated peeled fresh ginger
½ teaspoon grated lemon rind
8 frozen gluten-free waffles

1. Combine yogurt, ¼ cup sugar, and 2 teaspoons vanilla, stirring with a whisk. Set aside.

2. Combine berries and remaining 2 tablespoons sugar in a medium saucepan. Bring to a boil over medium heat, stirring constantly. Combine ¼ cup water and cornstarch in a small bowl, stirring until smooth; stir into berry mixture. Cook 1 minute or until thickened. Remove from heat; stir in remaining 1 teaspoon vanilla, ginger, and lemon rind. Cover and keep warm.

3. Toast waffles according to package directions. Serve waffles with berry sauce and yogurt mixture. **Yield: 4 servings (serving size: 2 waffles, ½ cup berry sauce, and ½ cup yogurt mixture).**

CALORIES 434; FAT 9.2g (sat 2.1g, mono 2.3g, poly 1.3g); PROTEIN 10.2g; CARB 80.1g; FIBER 5.1g; CHOL 6mg; IRON 0.9mg; SODIUM 429mg; CALC 117mg

Egg Crepes with Sausage

{Check for **Gluten**}

You'll want to prepare the filling first and keep it warm while you make the crepes.

Filling:
- 1 (12-ounce) package reduced-fat breakfast sausage
- ½ cup finely chopped onion
- 3 ounces fat-free cream cheese
- ¾ cup reduced-fat sour cream

Crepes:
- 1 large egg
- 4 large egg whites
- 3 tablespoons 1% low-fat milk
- Cooking spray
- Chopped fresh parsley (optional)

1. To prepare filling, cook sausage and onion in a large nonstick skillet over medium-high heat 9 minutes or until browned, stirring to crumble. Add cream cheese to sausage mixture, stirring until melted. Stir in sour cream. Remove pan from heat; cover and keep warm.

2. To prepare crepes, place egg, egg whites, and milk in a blender; process 15 seconds. Let stand 8 minutes.

3. Heat an 8-inch crepe pan or nonstick skillet over medium heat. Coat pan with cooking spray. Pour about 2 tablespoons egg mixture into center of pan; quickly tilt pan in all directions so batter covers pan with a thin film. Cook about 1 minute or until edges are dry, batter is almost set, and bottom is brown. Carefully lift edge of crepe with a spatula to test for doneness. Turn crepe over, and cook an additional 20 seconds. Remove to a plate. Repeat procedure 7 times with remaining batter.

4. Spoon about ¼ cup filling into center of the less-browned side of each crepe. Fold sides over filling; roll up. Place 2 filled crepes, seam sides up, on each of 4 serving plates. Garnish with chopped fresh parsley, if desired. Serve immediately. **Yield: 4 servings (serving size: 2 crepes).**

CALORIES 255; FAT 14.1g (sat 6.9g, mono 4.4g, poly 1.3g); PROTEIN 23.6g; CARB 7.3g; FIBER 0.3g; CHOL 127mg; IRON 1.6mg; SODIUM 749mg; CALC 167mg

Cooking Tip

The amount of batter needed is a little less than 2 tablespoons per crepe, so use shallow scoops of batter to ensure you get 8 crepes.

Eggs Blindfolded over Garlic-Cheddar Grits

Grits:
2½ cups hot cooked grits (such as Bob's Red Mill)
3 tablespoons shredded cheddar cheese
½ teaspoon garlic powder
½ teaspoon salt
½ teaspoon freshly ground black pepper

Eggs:
Cooking spray
4 large eggs, divided
½ cup ice cubes, divided
Freshly ground black pepper (optional)
Chopped fresh chives (optional)

1. To prepare grits, combine first 5 ingredients in a large bowl; keep warm.

2. To prepare eggs, heat a small skillet over medium heat. Coat pan with cooking spray. Break 2 eggs into pan; cook 1 minute or until whites are set. Add ¼ cup ice cubes to pan; cover and cook 2 minutes or until eggs are done. Remove from pan. Repeat procedure with remaining 2 eggs and ¼ cup ice. Serve eggs over grits. Garnish with black pepper and chives, if desired. **Yield: 4 servings (serving size: 1 egg and about ⅔ cup grits).**

CALORIES 184; FAT 7g (sat 2.7g, mono 2.5g, poly 0.9g); PROTEIN 9.8g; CARB 20.3g; FIBER 0.6g; CHOL 217mg; IRON 1.9mg; SODIUM 474mg; CALC 71mg

Cooking Tip

Blindfolded eggs are a short-order cook's version of poached eggs. The key is adding the ice cubes to the pan after the egg whites are set.

Ham and Cheese Strata

{Check for **Gluten**}

The longer this stands before baking, the more custardlike the consistency will be.

4 gluten-free English muffins,
 split, toasted, and cubed
8 Canadian bacon slices (such
 as Hormel), cut into 1-inch
 pieces
Cooking spray
1 cup (4 ounces) shredded
 reduced-fat sharp cheddar
 cheese
4 large eggs
8 large egg whites
3 cups 1% low-fat milk
1 teaspoon dry mustard
1 teaspoon Worcestershire
 sauce
½ teaspoon black pepper
½ teaspoon onion powder
¼ teaspoon hot pepper sauce
 (such as Tabasco)

1. Combine muffin cubes and Canadian bacon in a 13 x 9–inch baking dish coated with cooking spray; sprinkle with cheese.
2. Beat eggs and egg whites with a mixer at medium speed until blended. Add milk and next 5 ingredients, beating at low speed until blended. Pour egg mixture over muffin mixture. Cover and chill at least 2 hours or overnight.
3. Preheat oven to 350°.
4. Remove casserole from refrigerator, and let stand while oven preheats. Uncover casserole, and bake at 350° for 45 to 50 minutes or until browned. Let stand 15 minutes before serving.

Yield: 8 servings (serving size: ⅛ of casserole).

CALORIES 254; FAT 9.9g (sat 3.8g, mono 2.3g, poly 0.9g); PROTEIN 19.8g; CARB 27g; FIBER 1.1g; CHOL 134mg; IRON 2.4mg; SODIUM 821mg; CALC 331mg

Hearty Smoked Sausage Country Quiche

{Check for **Gluten**}

5 ounces gluten-free biscuit and baking mix (about 1½ cups; such as Bob's Red Mill)
2 tablespoons canola oil
3 tablespoons chilled butter, cut into cubes
¼ cup ice water
Cooking spray
6 ounces smoked turkey sausage, diced
1 cup chopped green bell pepper
1 cup chopped red bell pepper
½ cup diced yellow onion
2½ cups sliced yellow squash
½ teaspoon dried thyme
⅛ teaspoon crushed red pepper
2 tablespoons water
1 large egg
7 large egg whites
⅓ cup fat-free milk
6 tablespoons (1½ ounces) finely shredded reduced-fat sharp cheddar cheese

1. Preheat oven to 375°.
2. Weigh or lightly spoon baking mix into dry measuring cups; level with a knife. Combine baking mix and oil in a medium bowl. Cut in butter with a pastry blender or 2 knives until mixture resembles small peas. Add ice water, 1 tablespoon at a time, tossing with a fork until moist. Place between 2 sheets of plastic wrap; roll into an 11-inch circle. Place in a 9-inch deep-dish pie plate. Fold edges under and crimp; chill.
3. Heat a large nonstick skillet over medium-high heat. Coat pan with cooking spray. Add sausage to pan; cook 6 minutes or until browned, stirring frequently. Drain on paper towels.
4. Coat pan with cooking spray. Add bell peppers and onion; cook 3 minutes, stirring frequently. Stir in squash, thyme, and crushed red pepper. Coat vegetables with cooking spray; cook 4 minutes or until squash is almost tender, stirring frequently. Stir in 2 tablespoons water; cook 1 minute, scraping pan to loosen browned bits. Remove from heat; stir in sausage.
5. Combine egg, egg whites, and milk in a medium bowl, stirring well with a whisk. Spoon sausage mixture into prepared crust. Pour egg mixture over sausage mixture.
6. Bake at 375° for 35 minutes or until set. Remove from oven; sprinkle with cheese. Cut into 8 wedges. **Yield: 8 servings (serving size: 1 wedge).**

CALORIES 226; FAT 12.2g (sat 4.6g, mono 4.1g, poly 1.6g); PROTEIN 11.7g; CARB 18.1g; FIBER 2.4g; CHOL 53mg; IRON 3.3mg; SODIUM 498mg; CALC 160mg

The crust was by far my favorite element of the dish.
It was flaky and delicious and could be easily adapted for a variety of quiche recipes.

—Julia Monti

Egg and Cheese Breakfast Tacos with Homemade Salsa

{Check for **Gluten**}

Corn tortillas have a fraction of the sodium in flour ones, and they also contribute a pleasingly chewy texture. Round out breakfast with fresh mango slices.

1 cup chopped tomato
¼ cup chopped red onion
2 tablespoons chopped fresh cilantro
1 teaspoon minced jalapeño pepper
¼ teaspoon kosher salt
4 teaspoons fresh lime juice, divided
1 teaspoon minced garlic, divided
1 cup organic refried beans
¼ teaspoon ground cumin
1 tablespoon 1% low-fat milk
6 large eggs, lightly beaten
Cooking spray
¼ cup chopped green onions
8 (6-inch) corn tortillas
½ cup (2 ounces) shredded Monterey Jack cheese with jalapeño peppers
8 teaspoons reduced-fat sour cream

1. Combine first 5 ingredients in a small bowl. Stir in 2 teaspoons juice and ½ teaspoon garlic. Combine beans, remaining 2 teaspoons juice, remaining ½ teaspoon garlic, and cumin in another bowl.

2. Combine milk and eggs in a medium bowl; stir with a whisk. Heat a large nonstick skillet over medium-high heat. Coat pan with cooking spray. Add green onions to pan; sauté 1 minute, stirring frequently. Stir in egg mixture; cook 3 minutes or until soft-scrambled, stirring constantly. Remove from heat.

3. Warm tortillas according to package directions. Spread 1 tablespoon bean mixture on each tortilla. Spoon about 2 tablespoons egg mixture down center of each tortilla. Top each tortilla with 1 tablespoon tomato mixture, 1 tablespoon cheese, and 1 teaspoon sour cream. **Yield: 4 servings (serving size: 2 tacos).**

CALORIES 334; FAT 13.3g (sat 5.5g, mono 4.2g, poly 2.3g); PROTEIN 19g; CARB 34g; FIBER 6.5g; CHOL 289mg; IRON 2.9mg; SODIUM 407mg; CALC 201mg

Cooking Tip

Fresh-made salsa tastes more vibrant than bottled, and you control the added sodium, but you can also substitute fresh salsa from the grocery store, if you like. You'll find it in refrigerated tubs in the produce section.

Breakfast Tortilla

This hearty open-faced omelet, called a tortilla, uses potatoes inside instead of serving them on the side. This omelet maximizes flavor with Yukon gold potatoes, fresh tomatoes, and Manchego cheese.

½ pound Yukon gold potato (about 1 medium)
1 tablespoon minced fresh chives, divided
¾ teaspoon salt, divided
½ teaspoon freshly ground black pepper
4 large eggs
1 large egg white
1 tablespoon olive oil
1 garlic clove, minced
3 tablespoons finely grated Manchego cheese
1 teaspoon extra-virgin olive oil
½ cup halved grape or cherry tomatoes

1. Preheat oven to 350°.

2. Place potato in a saucepan; cover with water. Bring to a boil. Reduce heat, and simmer 20 minutes or until tender; drain. Cool. Peel potato; thinly slice.

3. Combine 2 teaspoons chives, ¼ teaspoon salt, pepper, eggs, and egg white in a bowl; stir with a whisk until blended.

4. Heat 1 tablespoon olive oil in an 8-inch ovenproof nonstick skillet over medium heat. Add garlic and potato slices; cook 30 seconds, gently turning potato to coat with oil. Sprinkle with remaining ½ teaspoon salt. Press potato mixture with a spatula into a solid layer in bottom of pan. Pour egg mixture over potato mixture; cook 1 minute. Gently stir egg and potato mixture. Press potato back down into bottom of pan; cook 2 minutes. Remove from heat. Sprinkle with cheese.

5. Bake at 350° for 7 minutes or until center is set. Remove from oven. Drizzle with 1 teaspoon extra-virgin olive oil. Loosen sides of tortilla from pan; gently slide onto a serving platter. Cut into 4 wedges. Top with tomatoes and remaining 1 teaspoon chives.

Yield: 4 servings (serving size: 1 wedge and 2 tablespoons tomatoes).

CALORIES 190; FAT 10.7g (sat 2.8g, mono 5.5g, poly 1.2g); PROTEIN 10g; CARB 14g; FIBER 1.2g; CHOL 215mg; IRON 1.3mg; SODIUM 581mg; CALC 77mg

Cilantro-Pear Turkey Breakfast Sausage

☑ Dairy **free**

Making your own breakfast sausage is easier than you might think. Pear adds a subtle sweetness to this spiced breakfast side. Serve with eggs and fruit to complete the meal.

- 1 pound ground turkey breast
- ¾ cup diced unpeeled pear
- ¾ cup finely chopped red bell pepper
- ½ cup finely chopped red onion
- ¼ cup chopped fresh cilantro
- 1 teaspoon dried rubbed sage
- ½ teaspoon salt
- ½ teaspoon ground cumin
- ½ teaspoon ground allspice
- ½ teaspoon crushed red pepper
- 1 tablespoon canola oil, divided

1. Combine first 10 ingredients in a medium bowl. Shape into 8 (½-inch-thick) patties. Heat 1½ teaspoons oil in a large nonstick skillet over medium heat. Add 4 patties; cook 4 minutes. Turn patties over, and cook 3 minutes or until done. Remove patties from pan; drain on paper towels. Repeat procedure with remaining oil and remaining patties. **Yield: 4 servings (serving size: 2 patties).**

CALORIES 192; FAT 5.3g (sat 0.8g, mono 2.5g, poly 1.5g); PROTEIN 27.1g; CARB 9.2g; FIBER 2.3g; CHOL 46mg; IRON 1.1mg; SODIUM 375mg; CALC 18mg

Banana Breakfast Smoothie

This protein-packed smoothie is perfect for breakfast on the go. Adding the yogurt at the very end imparts a creamy texture.

½ cup 1% low-fat milk
½ cup crushed ice
1 tablespoon honey
⅛ teaspoon ground nutmeg
1 frozen sliced ripe large banana
1 cup plain 2% reduced-fat Greek yogurt

1. Combine first 5 ingredients in a blender; process 2 minutes or until smooth. Add yogurt; process just until blended. Serve immediately. **Yield: 2 servings (serving size: 1 cup).**

CALORIES 212; FAT 3.6g (sat 2.5g, mono 0.2g, poly 0.1g); PROTEIN 14.2g; CARB 34.2g; FIBER 2g; CHOL 9mg; IRON 0.3mg; SODIUM 75mg; CALC 200mg

Peach-Mango Smoothie:

Place ⅔ cup frozen sliced peaches, ⅔ cup frozen mango pieces, ⅔ cup peach nectar, 1 tablespoon honey, and 1 (6-ounce) carton organic peach fat-free yogurt in a blender; process 2 minutes or until smooth. Serve immediately. **Yield: 2 servings (serving size: 1 cup).**

CALORIES 184; FAT 0.3g (sat 0.1g, mono 0.1g, poly 0.1g); PROTEIN 4.1g; CARB 44g; FIBER 2.4g; CHOL 2mg; IRON 0.4mg; SODIUM 50mg; CALC 107mg

Strawberry-Guava Smoothie:

Place 1 cup quartered strawberries (about 5 ounces), ½ cup guava nectar, 1 (6-ounce) carton organic strawberry fat-free yogurt, 1 frozen sliced ripe small banana, and 5 ice cubes (about 2 ounces) in a blender; process 2 minutes or until smooth. Serve immediately. **Yield: 2 servings (serving size: 1 cup).**

CALORIES 91; FAT 0.4g (sat 0.1g, mono 0g, poly 0.1g); PROTEIN 1g; CARB 21.6g; FIBER 1.4g; CHOL 0mg; IRON 2mg; SODIUM 16mg; CALC 41mg

Main Dishes

Tabbouleh-Style Amaranth Salad

1½ cups cold water
½ cup uncooked whole-grain amaranth (such as Arrowhead Mills)
 2 cups diced unpeeled English cucumber
½ cup thinly sliced celery
½ cup finely chopped red onion
¼ cup chopped fresh mint
¼ cup chopped fresh flat-leaf parsley
¼ cup pine nuts, toasted
 2 tablespoons extra-virgin olive oil
 1 teaspoon grated lemon rind
 2 tablespoons fresh lemon juice
¼ teaspoon salt
¼ teaspoon crushed red pepper
½ cup drained no-salt-added canned chickpeas (garbanzo beans)
 1 cup (4 ounces) feta cheese, crumbled
Lemon wedges (optional)

1. Bring 1½ cups cold water and amaranth to a boil in a medium saucepan; reduce heat, cover, and simmer 20 minutes or until water is almost absorbed (it will have the appearance of mush).
2. While amaranth cooks, combine cucumber and next 11 ingredients in a large bowl.
3. Place amaranth in a sieve, and rinse under cold running water until room temperature; drain well, pressing with the back of a spoon. Add to cucumber mixture; toss to blend. Add cheese; toss gently. Garnish with lemon wedges, if desired. **Yield: 4 servings (serving size: 1¼ cups).**

CALORIES 323; FAT 20.5g (sat 6g, mono 8g, poly 4.2g); PROTEIN 10.9g; CARB 26.7g; FIBER 3g; CHOL 25mg; IRON 3.5mg; SODIUM 493mg; CALC 220mg

Cooking Tip

It's important that the amaranth is placed in a fine mesh sieve. The grain is so tiny that it will slip through a traditional strainer. If one is not available, place the cooked amaranth on a large baking sheet, and spread it in a thin layer so it will cool without clumping together.

Chickpea Bajane

☑ Dairy **free**
{Check for **Gluten**}

Bajane is a Provençal term for the midday meal. Chickpeas are a staple in Provence, where they are often stewed and served with pasta and vegetables. In this version, chickpeas, leeks, carrots, fennel, and spinach are served atop protein-rich quinoa.

4 teaspoons extra-virgin olive oil, divided
1 garlic clove, minced
2 cups organic vegetable broth, divided
1 cup water
1 cup uncooked quinoa
5½ teaspoons chopped fresh thyme, divided
½ teaspoon salt, divided
2 cups thinly sliced leek (about 1 large)
4 garlic cloves, chopped
2½ cups sliced fennel bulb (about 1 large)
1¾ cups (¼-inch-thick) slices carrot (about ¾ pound)
½ teaspoon fennel seeds
½ cup white wine
1 (15-ounce) can no-salt-added chickpeas (garbanzo beans), rinsed and drained
1 tablespoon fresh lemon juice
¼ teaspoon freshly ground black pepper
1 (6-ounce) package fresh baby spinach

1. Heat 2 teaspoons oil in a large saucepan over medium-high heat. Add 1 minced garlic clove to pan; sauté 1 minute. Add 1 cup broth, 1 cup water, quinoa, 1½ teaspoons thyme, and ¼ teaspoon salt. Cover, reduce heat, and simmer 15 minutes or until liquid is absorbed and quinoa is tender. Remove from heat; fluff with a fork.

2. Heat 1 teaspoon oil in a Dutch oven over medium-high heat. Add leek and 4 chopped garlic cloves to pan; sauté 5 minutes or until tender. Add remaining 1 teaspoon oil, fennel bulb, carrot, and fennel seeds; sauté 10 minutes or until vegetables are golden. Add wine; cook 3 minutes or until liquid almost evaporates. Stir in remaining 1 cup broth, 2 teaspoons thyme, and chickpeas; cook 1 minute or until thoroughly heated. Remove from heat; stir in juice, remaining ¼ teaspoon salt, pepper, and spinach.

3. Place about ⅔ cup quinoa in each of 4 bowls; top each serving with about 1½ cups chickpea mixture. Sprinkle each serving with ½ teaspoon thyme. **Yield: 4 servings.**

CALORIES 357; FAT 7.8g (sat 0.7g, mono 4.4g, poly 1.9g); PROTEIN 11.8g; CARB 60.4g; FIBER 11.3g; CHOL 0mg; IRON 5.9mg; SODIUM 728mg; CALC 168mg

Curried Quinoa Salad with Cucumber-Mint Raita

This Indian-inspired dish features quinoa, a high-protein grain that cooks relatively quickly. We like the heat that Madras curry powder brings, but use regular curry powder, if you prefer.

1 teaspoon olive oil
2 teaspoons Madras curry powder
1 garlic clove, crushed
1 cup uncooked quinoa
2 cups water
¾ teaspoon kosher salt
1 diced peeled ripe mango
½ cup diced celery
¼ cup thinly sliced green onions
3 tablespoons chopped fresh cilantro
3 tablespoons currants
¼ cup finely diced peeled English cucumber
2 teaspoons chopped fresh mint
1 (6-ounce) carton plain low-fat yogurt
1 (6-ounce) package fresh baby spinach

1. Heat oil in a medium saucepan over medium-high heat. Add curry powder and garlic to pan; cook 1 minute, stirring constantly. Add quinoa and 2 cups water; bring to a boil. Cover, reduce heat, and simmer 16 minutes or until tender. Remove from heat; stir in salt. Cool completely.

2. Add mango and next 4 ingredients to cooled quinoa; toss gently.

3. Combine cucumber, mint, and yogurt in a small bowl; stir well. Divide spinach evenly among 6 plates, and top each serving with about ¾ cup quinoa mixture and about 2 tablespoons raita. **Yield: 6 servings.**

CALORIES 268; FAT 4.5g (sat 0.9g, mono 1.9g, poly 1.3g); PROTEIN 10.7g; CARB 46.8g; FIBER 6g; CHOL 2mg; IRON 4.4mg; SODIUM 418mg; CALC 122mg

Yang Chow Fried Rice

☑ Dairy **free**
{Check for **Gluten**}

This is a vegetarian version of the classic Chinese dish that traditionally includes shrimp and ham. The fried rice can stand alone as a one-dish meal; however, if you desire a crunchy side, Sesame-Soy Snow Peas fills the bill. Cut the cilantro into small sprigs instead of chopping for a pretty garnish.

2 tablespoons canola oil, divided
4 large eggs, lightly beaten and divided
¼ teaspoon freshly ground black pepper, divided
Dash of salt
1¾ cups thinly sliced green onions, divided
2 teaspoons grated peeled fresh ginger
2 garlic cloves, minced
5 cups cooked short-grain rice, chilled
¼ cup lower-sodium soy sauce
½ teaspoon salt
1 (10-ounce) package frozen green peas, thawed
3 tablespoons chopped fresh cilantro

1. Heat 2 teaspoons oil in a large nonstick skillet over medium-high heat. Add half of eggs; swirl to coat bottom of pan evenly. Sprinkle with ⅛ teaspoon pepper and dash of salt; cook 3 minutes or until egg is done. Remove egg from pan; thinly slice, and set aside.

2. Wipe pan clean with a paper towel. Heat remaining 4 teaspoons oil in pan over medium-high heat. Add 1 cup onions, ginger, and garlic; stir-fry 30 seconds. Add remaining eggs and rice; stir-fry 3 minutes. Stir in half of reserved egg strips, remaining ¾ cup onions, remaining ⅛ teaspoon pepper, soy sauce, ½ teaspoon salt, and peas; cook 30 seconds, stirring well to combine. Top with remaining egg strips and cilantro. **Yield: 6 servings (serving size: about 1 cup).**

CALORIES 348; FAT 8.5g (sat 1.5g, mono 4.1g, poly 2g); PROTEIN 11g; CARB 55g; FIBER 4.9g; CHOL 141mg; IRON 3.9mg; SODIUM 683mg; CALC 34mg

Sesame-Soy Snow Peas:

Steam 4 cups trimmed snow peas 2 minutes or until crisp-tender. Combine 2 tablespoons lower-sodium soy sauce, 1 tablespoon dark sesame oil, and ¼ teaspoon freshly ground black pepper in a large bowl. Add snow peas; toss to coat. **Yield: 6 servings.**

CALORIES 70; FAT 2.5g (sat 0.4g, mono 1g, poly 1.1g); PROTEIN 3.4g; CARB 8.7g; FIBER 2.9g; CHOL 0mg; IRON 2.3mg; SODIUM 206mg; CALC 48mg

Soft Tacos with Green Chile–Cilantro Rice and Egg

☑ Dairy **free**
{Check for **Gluten**}

This versatile dish can be served for breakfast, lunch, or dinner.

3 tablespoons fat-free milk
6 large egg whites
2 large eggs
¼ cup finely chopped red onion
¼ cup chopped tomato
¼ cup chopped fresh cilantro
1 tablespoon extra-virgin olive oil
½ teaspoon ground cumin
¼ teaspoon salt
1 (4.5-ounce) can chopped green chiles, undrained
1 cup hot cooked brown rice
Cooking spray
8 corn tortillas
4 lime wedges (optional)

1. Combine first 3 ingredients in a medium bowl, stirring with a whisk.

2. Combine onion and next 6 ingredients in another medium bowl, stirring with a spoon. Add rice; stir gently. Cover and keep warm.

3. Heat a large nonstick skillet over medium heat. Coat pan with cooking spray. Add egg mixture to pan; cook over medium heat 2 minutes. Do not stir until mixture begins to set on bottom. Draw a heat-resistant spatula through egg mixture to form large curds. Do not stir constantly. Egg mixture is done when thickened, but still moist. Remove from heat.

4. Warm tortillas according to package directions. Spoon scrambled egg evenly over tortillas; top evenly with rice mixture, and fold in half. Serve with lime wedges, if desired. **Yield: 4 servings (serving size: 2 tacos).**

CALORIES 309; FAT 8.8g (sat 1.4g, mono 4.5g, poly 1.8g); PROTEIN 12.3g; CARB 44.2g; FIBER 3.3g; CHOL 106mg; IRON 0.9mg; SODIUM 758mg; CALC 42mg

Pan-Fried Catfish with Cajun Tartar Sauce

☑ Dairy **free**

Cooking spray
4 (6-ounce) farm-raised catfish fillets
2 teaspoons Cajun seasoning
⅛ teaspoon salt
½ cup fat-free mayonnaise
1 tablespoon sweet pickle relish
1 tablespoon minced fresh onion
1 tablespoon capers, drained
1 teaspoon hot pepper sauce (such as Tabasco)
¼ teaspoon dried oregano

1. Heat a large nonstick skillet over medium-high heat; coat with cooking spray. Sprinkle fish evenly with Cajun seasoning and salt. Add 2 fillets to pan; cook 4 minutes on each side or until desired degree of doneness. Remove fish from pan, and keep warm. Wipe pan clean with paper towels; recoat with cooking spray. Repeat procedure with remaining 2 fillets.

2. While fish cooks, combine mayonnaise and next 5 ingredients in a small bowl. Serve with fish. **Yield: 4 servings (serving size: 1 fillet and about 3 tablespoons tartar sauce).**

CALORIES 262; FAT 13.9g (sat 3.2g, mono 6.1g, poly 2.7g); PROTEIN 26.7g; CARB 6.3g; FIBER 1g; CHOL 83mg; IRON 1mg; SODIUM 742mg; CALC 20mg

Cider-Mustard Slaw:

Combine half of 1 (16-ounce) package cabbage-and-carrot coleslaw, 1 tablespoon brown sugar, 2 tablespoons cider vinegar, 1 tablespoon stone-ground mustard, and ⅛ teaspoon salt. **Yield: 4 servings.**

CALORIES 31; FAT 0g (sat 0g, mono 0g, poly 0g); PROTEIN 0.7g; CARB 6.8g; FIBER 1.3g; CHOL 0mg; IRON 0mg; SODIUM 136mg; CALC 3mg

Cooking Tip

Instead of a traditional crunchy coating, we used a Cajun spice blend to season the fish and pan-fried it in a pan coated with cooking spray, which helps keep calories in check and is less involved than deep-fat frying. For a spicier sauce, add more hot pepper sauce.

Pan-Roasted Grouper with Provençal Vegetables

{Check for **Gluten**}

Use a broiler pan for both components of this recipe. The fennel-tomato mixture cooks in the bottom of the pan, helping to steam the fish on the rack above.

2 cups thinly sliced fennel bulb (about 1 medium bulb)
2 tablespoons fresh orange juice
16 picholine olives, pitted and chopped
1 (28-ounce) can no-salt-added whole tomatoes, drained and coarsely chopped
½ teaspoon salt, divided
½ teaspoon black pepper, divided
 Cooking spray
2 teaspoons olive oil
1 garlic clove, minced
4 (6-ounce) grouper fillets (about 1 inch thick)

1. Preheat oven to 450°.
2. Combine first 4 ingredients. Add ¼ teaspoon salt and ¼ teaspoon pepper; toss well. Spoon mixture into bottom of a broiler pan coated with cooking spray. Bake at 450° for 10 minutes; stir once.
3. Combine remaining ¼ teaspoon salt, remaining ¼ teaspoon pepper, oil, and garlic; brush evenly over fish. Remove pan from oven. Place fish on broiler pan rack coated with cooking spray; place rack over fennel mixture.
4. Bake at 450° for 10 minutes or until desired degree of doneness. **Yield: 4 servings (serving size: 1 fillet and ¾ cup vegetables).**

CALORIES 236; FAT 6g (sat 1g, mono 3.2g, poly 1g); PROTEIN 34.9g; CARB 10.8g; FIBER 3.3g; CHOL 63mg; IRON 3.4mg; SODIUM 587mg; CALC 122mg

Spinach-Mushroom Salad:

Combine 6 cups torn spinach, 1 cup sliced mushrooms, and ½ cup thinly sliced red onion in a large bowl. Combine ⅓ cup fat-free ranch dressing, ¼ cup (1 ounce) grated fresh Parmesan cheese, if desired, and ½ teaspoon freshly ground black pepper in a small bowl; spoon over salad. Toss gently to coat. **Yield: 4 servings.**

CALORIES 53; FAT 0.5g (sat 0.1g, mono 0g, poly 0.1g); PROTEIN 2.2g; CARB 10.9g; FIBER 1.6g; CHOL 0mg; IRON 1.4mg; SODIUM 273mg; CALC 55mg

Grilled Halibut with Three-Pepper Relish

☑ Dairy **free**

For a complete meal, pair this dish with steamed green beans tossed with olive oil, salt, and freshly ground black pepper and topped with pine nuts.

Relish:
- 1 yellow bell pepper, quartered
- 1 red bell pepper, quartered
- 1 orange bell pepper, quartered
- Cooking spray
- 2 tablespoons chopped fresh parsley
- 2 tablespoons chopped capers
- 1 tablespoon olive oil
- 1 tablespoon balsamic vinegar
- ¼ teaspoon kosher salt
- ¼ teaspoon black pepper
- 1 garlic clove, minced

Fish:
- 1 tablespoon olive oil
- 8 (6-ounce) skinless halibut fillets
- 2 teaspoons chopped fresh thyme
- ¾ teaspoon kosher salt
- ½ teaspoon freshly ground black pepper

1. Preheat grill to medium-high heat.

2. To prepare relish, coat bell pepper pieces with cooking spray. Place pepper pieces on grill rack; grill 3 minutes on each side or until lightly charred. Remove from grill; cool slightly. Coarsely chop bell pepper pieces. Combine chopped bell peppers, parsley, and next 6 ingredients; set aside.

3. To prepare fish, brush 1 tablespoon oil evenly over fish. Sprinkle fish evenly with thyme, ¾ teaspoon salt, and ½ teaspoon black pepper. Place fish on grill rack; grill 4 minutes on each side or until desired degree of doneness. Serve with relish.

Yield: 8 servings (serving size: 1 fillet and ¼ cup relish).

CALORIES 224; FAT 7.3g (sat 1g, mono 3.7g, poly 1.6g); PROTEIN 34.6g; CARB 3.5g; FIBER 1.1g; CHOL 52mg; IRON 1.8mg; SODIUM 392mg; CALC 85mg

Indian-Spiced Salmon

 Dairy **free**

½ teaspoon ground ginger
½ teaspoon garam masala
½ teaspoon ground coriander
¼ teaspoon ground turmeric
 Dash of kosher salt
 Dash of ground red pepper
4 (6-ounce) skinless salmon
  fillets
 Cooking spray

1. Preheat broiler.
2. Combine first 6 ingredients. Rub spice mixture evenly over fillets. Place fillets on a broiler pan or baking sheet coated with cooking spray. Cover with foil; broil 7 minutes. Remove foil; broil an additional 4 minutes or until desired degree of doneness.
Yield: 4 servings (serving size: 1 fillet).

CALORIES 242; FAT 9.8g (sat 1.6g, mono 3.1g, poly 4.1g); PROTEIN 38.4g; CARB 0.4g; FIBER 0.1g; CHOL 99mg; IRON 1.1mg; SODIUM 129mg; CALC 10mg

Nutty Basmati Rice:

Bring 2 cups water to a boil in a small saucepan. Stir in 1 cup uncooked basmati rice and ¼ teaspoon salt; cover, reduce heat, and cook 20 minutes or until rice is tender. Remove from heat; stir in 3 tablespoons chopped fresh flat-leaf parsley and 4 teaspoons dry-roasted salted cashew pieces. Keep warm. **Yield: 4 servings (serving size: ½ cup).**

CALORIES 97; FAT 1.4g (sat 0.3g, mono 0.8g, poly 0.2g); PROTEIN 2g; CARB 19.1g; FIBER 0.4g; CHOL 0mg; IRON 0.5mg; SODIUM 147mg; CALC 5mg

The Indian-Spiced Salmon and Nutty Basmati Rice were both great! They were easy to prepare and did not require a lot of time. I simply cooked some fresh green beans to go with these two dishes, and we had an easy, complete meal. My family loved them. Oh, and of course no one noticed that it did not have gluten.

—*Connie Hendon*

Sole with Tarragon-Butter Sauce

{Check for **Gluten**}

This recipe is quick enough for a weeknight meal but special enough for company. Serve with green beans.

- 4 (6-ounce) sole fillets
- ½ teaspoon salt, divided
- ¼ teaspoon freshly ground black pepper
- Cooking spray
- ¾ cup dry white wine
- ¾ cup fat-free, lower-sodium chicken broth
- ⅓ cup finely chopped shallots
- 1 tablespoon minced fresh garlic
- 5 teaspoons butter, cut into small pieces
- 1 tablespoon chopped fresh chives
- 1½ teaspoons chopped fresh tarragon

1. Sprinkle fish with ¼ teaspoon salt and pepper. Heat a large nonstick skillet over medium-high heat; coat pan with cooking spray. Add 2 fillets to pan; cook 2 minutes on each side or until desired degree of doneness. Remove from pan; cover and keep warm. Repeat procedure with remaining fish.

2. Add wine and next 3 ingredients to pan; bring to a boil. Reduce heat, and simmer until reduced to about ½ cup (about 10 minutes). Remove from heat; stir in remaining ¼ teaspoon salt, butter, chives, and tarragon. Spoon sauce over fish; serve immediately. **Yield: 4 servings (serving size: 1 fillet and 3 tablespoons sauce).**

CALORIES 197; FAT 6.6g (sat 3.4g, mono 1.6g, poly 1g); PROTEIN 29.4g; CARB 3.4g; FIBER 0.4g; CHOL 92mg; IRON 0.8mg; SODIUM 528mg; CALC 38mg

Rice Amandine:

Melt 2 teaspoons butter in a medium saucepan over medium-high heat. Add 1 cup long-grain rice; sauté 1 minute. Add 2 cups fat-free, lower-sodium chicken broth. Cover, reduce heat, and simmer 15 minutes or until rice is tender. Stir in ¼ cup chopped fresh parsley and 2 tablespoons toasted sliced almonds. **Yield: 4 servings.**

CALORIES 206; FAT 3.7g (sat 1.4g, mono 1.5g, poly 0.5g); PROTEIN 4.5g; CARB 37.8g; FIBER 1.1g; CHOL 5mg; IRON 2.3mg; SODIUM 243mg; CALC 26mg

Seared Scallops with Farmers' Market Salad

☑ Dairy **free**

Look for dry-packed scallops, which will brown best.

2 cups chopped tomato (about 1 pound)
1 cup chopped fresh basil
¾ teaspoon kosher salt, divided
¼ teaspoon freshly ground black pepper, divided
1 tablespoon canola oil
1½ pounds sea scallops
Cooking spray
2 cups fresh corn kernels (about 3 ears)

1. Combine tomato, basil, ¼ teaspoon salt, and ⅛ teaspoon pepper; toss gently. Set aside.

2. Heat a large cast-iron or other heavy skillet over high heat. Add oil to pan, swirling to coat. Pat scallops dry with paper towels; sprinkle with remaining ½ teaspoon salt and remaining ⅛ teaspoon pepper. Add scallops to pan; cook 2 minutes or until browned. Turn scallops; cook 2 minutes or until done. Remove scallops from pan; keep warm.

3. Coat pan with cooking spray. Add corn to pan; sauté 2 minutes or until lightly browned. Add to tomato mixture; toss gently. Serve salad with scallops. **Yield: 4 servings (serving size: about 3 scallops and about 1 cup salad).**

CALORIES 251; FAT 5.7g (sat 0.5g, mono 2.4g, poly 1.9g); PROTEIN 31.6g; CARB 19.4g; FIBER 3.3g; CHOL 56mg; IRON 1.4mg; SODIUM 641mg; CALC 70mg

Cooking Tip

Be sure you buy dry-packed scallops. Scallops marked "wet packed" have been treated with a liquid solution containing sodium tripolyphosphate. The scallops absorb the salty mixture and plump up, resulting in a heavier weight and a higher market price. But when you cook them, the liquid portion will cook out, leaving you with smaller scallops and a higher sodium content.

Pan-Seared Scallops with Bacon and Spinach

☑ Dairy **free**

3 center-cut bacon slices
1½ pounds jumbo sea scallops (about 12)
¼ teaspoon kosher salt, divided
¼ teaspoon freshly ground black pepper, divided
1 cup chopped onion
6 garlic cloves, sliced
12 ounces fresh baby spinach
4 lemon wedges (optional)

1. Cook bacon in a large cast-iron skillet over medium-high heat until crisp. Remove bacon from pan, reserving 1 tablespoon drippings in pan; coarsely chop bacon, and set aside. Increase heat to high.

2. Pat scallops dry with paper towels. Sprinkle scallops evenly with ⅛ teaspoon salt and ⅛ teaspoon pepper. Add scallops to drippings in pan; cook 2½ minutes on each side or until done. Transfer to a plate; keep warm. Reduce heat to medium-high. Add onion and garlic to pan; sauté 3 minutes, stirring frequently. Add half of spinach; cook 1 minute, stirring frequently. Add remaining half of spinach; cook 2 minutes or just until wilted, stirring frequently. Remove from heat; stir in remaining ⅛ teaspoon salt and remaining ⅛ teaspoon pepper. Divide spinach mixture among 4 plates; top each serving evenly with chopped bacon and 3 scallops. Serve immediately with lemon wedges, if desired. **Yield: 4 servings (serving size: 3 scallops and ¾ cup spinach).**

CALORIES 315; FAT 5.8g (sat 1.7g, mono 1.5g, poly 0.4g); PROTEIN 45.3g; CARB 21.9g; FIBER 4.8g; CHOL 106mg; IRON 6.7mg; SODIUM 758mg; CALC 139mg

Cooking Tip

Scallops cooked in a pan are always in danger of being steamed rather than seared, so be sure to use a big pan and high heat. A cast-iron skillet is ideal since it gets really hot and can handle high temperatures, unlike a nonstick skillet, which has a more delicate nonstick coating that can only handle up to medium-high heat.

Mango Shrimp Kebabs

These fresh-flavored kebabs are a great option for entertaining.

1½ **pounds peeled and deveined large shrimp**
½ **teaspoon salt**
⅛ **teaspoon freshly ground black pepper**
2 **large red bell peppers, cut into 1-inch pieces**
2 **mangoes, peeled and cut into 1-inch cubes**
1 **small red onion, cut into 1-inch pieces**
Cooking spray
2 **limes, cut into wedges**

1. Preheat grill to medium-high heat.
2. Sprinkle shrimp evenly with salt and pepper. Thread shrimp, bell pepper, mango, and onion pieces alternately onto each of 8 (12-inch) skewers. Place skewers on grill rack coated with cooking spray; grill 2 minutes on each side or until shrimp are done. Squeeze juice from lime wedges over kebabs. **Yield: 4 servings (serving size: 2 skewers).**

CALORIES 277; FAT 3.3g (sat 0.7g, mono 0.5g, poly 1.2g); PROTEIN 35.8g; CARB 27.1g; FIBER 4.2g; CHOL 259mg; IRON 4.5mg; SODIUM 551mg; CALC 109mg

Cooking Tip

Skewering small chunks of food on wooden sticks or thin metal rods is a grilling tradition. Soak wooden skewers in water for at least 30 minutes before using them on the grill or they'll burn, and discard them after use. Metal skewers can be reused and require no soaking.

It was a hit and not as difficult as I first thought. This recipe will be a good one to serve when I have another couple over for dinner.

—Anita Royse

Greek Shrimp and Asparagus Risotto

{Check for **Gluten**}

If you don't have dill on hand, chopped fresh flat-leaf parsley or chives will also work in this dish.

{

- 3 cups fat-free, lower-sodium chicken broth
- 1 cup water
- 2 teaspoons olive oil
- 2¾ cups chopped Vidalia or other sweet onion (about 2 medium)
- 1 cup Arborio rice or other medium-grain rice
- 2 garlic cloves, minced
- 1¾ cups (½-inch) slices asparagus (about 8 ounces)
- 1 pound peeled and deveined medium shrimp, cut into 1-inch pieces
- ½ cup (2 ounces) crumbled feta cheese
- 1 tablespoon chopped fresh dill
- 2 tablespoons fresh lemon juice
- ⅛ teaspoon salt
- ⅛ teaspoon freshly ground black pepper

1. Bring broth and 1 cup water to a simmer in a medium saucepan (do not boil). Keep warm over low heat.

2. Heat oil in a large saucepan over medium-high heat. Add onion to pan; sauté 5 minutes or until tender. Stir in rice and garlic; sauté 1 minute. Add broth mixture, ½ cup at a time, stirring constantly until each portion of broth is absorbed before adding the next (about 30 minutes total).

3. Stir in asparagus and shrimp; cook 5 minutes or until shrimp are done, stirring constantly. Remove from heat; stir in cheese and remaining ingredients. **Yield: 4 servings (serving size: 1½ cups).**

CALORIES 426; FAT 8.9g (sat 3.6g, mono 2.8g, poly 1.2g); PROTEIN 33g; CARB 53.5g; FIBER 5.1g; CHOL 189mg; IRON 4.5mg; SODIUM 794mg; CALC 194 mg

Fennel Salad:

Combine 2 tablespoons fresh lemon juice, 1 tablespoon olive oil, ¼ teaspoon salt, ¼ teaspoon crushed fennel seeds, and ⅛ teaspoon freshly ground black pepper in a large bowl. Add 6 cups torn romaine lettuce and 1 cup thinly sliced fennel bulb; toss well to coat. **Yield: 4 servings.**

CALORIES 51; FAT 3.7g (sat 0.5g, mono 2.5g, poly 0.5g); PROTEIN 1.2g; CARB 4.7g; FIBER 2.3g; CHOL 0mg; IRON 0.9mg; SODIUM 163mg; CALC 36mg

Sirloin Steak with Merlot-Balsamic Reduction

☑ Dairy **free**
{Check for **Gluten**}

Marinating the steak and cutting it on the diagonal after cooking ensure tenderness. Serve with steamed asparagus and mashed red potatoes to round out the meal.

½ **cup merlot**
2 **tablespoons balsamic vinegar**
1 **tablespoon Worcestershire sauce**
½ **teaspoon coarsely ground black pepper**
¼ **teaspoon salt**
1 **(1-pound) boneless sirloin steak (½ inch thick), trimmed**
Cooking spray
1 **tablespoon canola oil**
½ **cup finely chopped shallots (about 3 medium)**

1. Combine first 5 ingredients in a large heavy-duty zip-top plastic bag. Add steak to bag; seal. Marinate at room temperature 15 minutes, turning frequently.

2. Heat a large nonstick skillet over medium-high heat. Coat pan with cooking spray. Remove steak from bag, reserving marinade. Add steak to pan; cook 3 minutes on each side. Reduce heat to medium; cook an additional 3 minutes on each side or until desired degree of doneness. Remove steak from pan; cover and keep warm.

3. Add oil to pan. Add shallots; cook 2 minutes or until shallots begin to brown, stirring frequently. Stir in reserved marinade, scraping pan to loosen browned bits. Increase heat, and bring to a boil; boil 1 to 2 minutes or until reduced to ¼ cup.

4. Cut steak diagonally across grain into thin slices. Place steak slices and any accumulated juices on a serving platter. Spoon sauce over steak. **Yield: 4 servings (serving size: 3 ounces steak and 4 teaspoons sauce).**

CALORIES 196; FAT 8g (sat 2g, mono 4g, poly 1.2g); PROTEIN 23g; CARB 6.6g; FIBER 0.1g; CHOL 42mg; IRON 2.2mg; SODIUM 268mg; CALC 35mg

Filet Mignon with Fresh Herb and Garlic Rub

☑ Dairy **free**

The filet mignon comes from the small end of the tenderloin. Serve with roasted red potato wedges and steamed broccoli florets. Place florets in a microwave-safe bowl with a little water; cover with wax paper, and microwave at HIGH 3 minutes or until crisp-tender.

2 teaspoons bottled minced garlic
1½ teaspoons minced fresh basil
1½ teaspoons minced fresh thyme
1½ teaspoons minced fresh rosemary
½ teaspoon salt
¼ teaspoon black pepper
4 (4-ounce) beef tenderloin steaks (1 inch thick), trimmed
Cooking spray

1. Combine first 6 ingredients in a small bowl; rub evenly over steaks.

2. Heat a large nonstick skillet over medium-high heat. Coat pan with cooking spray. Add steaks to pan, and cook 4 minutes on each side or until desired degree of doneness. **Yield: 4 servings (serving size: 1 steak).**

CALORIES 189; FAT 8.8g (sat 3.2g, mono 3.2g, poly 0.3g); PROTEIN 24.1g; CARB 0.8g; FIBER 0.2g; CHOL 71mg; IRON 3.1mg; SODIUM 349mg; CALC 9mg

Spicy Asian-Marinated Flank Steak

☑ Dairy **free**
{Check for **Gluten**}

Pair this spicy entrée with snap peas and chopped red bell pepper.

{ 2 tablespoons lower-sodium soy sauce
  1 tablespoon fresh lime juice
  1 teaspoon curry powder
  1 teaspoon ground red pepper
  2 teaspoons minced peeled fresh ginger
  1½ teaspoons rice wine vinegar
  1 teaspoon olive oil
  1 teaspoon dark sesame oil
  1 (8-ounce) can crushed pineapple in juice, drained
  4 garlic cloves, minced
  1 (1-pound) flank steak, trimmed
  Cooking spray
  ¼ teaspoon salt

1. Combine first 10 ingredients in a large zip-top plastic bag. Add steak to bag; seal. Marinate in refrigerator 24 hours, turning occasionally.

2. Preheat grill to medium-high heat.

3. Remove steak from bag; discard marinade. Place steak on grill rack coated with cooking spray, and grill 4 minutes on each side or until desired degree of doneness. Sprinkle with salt, and let stand 5 minutes. Cut steak diagonally across grain into thin slices. **Yield: 4 servings (serving size: 3 ounces).**

CALORIES 236; FAT 8.6g (sat 3.2g, mono 3.6g, poly 0.7g); PROTEIN 32.2g; CARB 5.9g; FIBER 0.5g; CHOL 49mg; IRON 2.2mg; SODIUM 365mg; CALC 32mg

Cooking Tip

This spicy Asian marinade is versatile enough to apply to a variety of meats. Try it with pork tenderloin and cuts of chicken.

Cooking Tip

Keep this flavorful Basic Breading Mix for Fried Foods on hand in your pantry, and you'll always be ready to quickly fry up meats or vegetables for a tasty treat. Remember, any mix that touches raw meat, poultry, or fish has to be discarded, so transfer the amount you need to a plate or shallow bowl so you don't contaminate the remaining mix.

Chicken-Fried Steak with Soy Milk Gravy

☑ Dairy **free**

Be sure to buy regular soy milk, not light, for the best results. You can also use cow's milk or hemp milk in this recipe.

1 cup Basic Breading Mix for Fried Foods
2 cups plain soy milk, divided
2 large eggs
4 (4-ounce) cubed steaks
Cooking spray
2 tablespoons canola oil, divided
1 tablespoon cornstarch
½ teaspoon salt
½ teaspoon freshly ground black pepper
4 teaspoons chopped fresh parsley

1. Place Basic Breading Mix for Fried Foods in a shallow bowl. Combine ½ cup soy milk and eggs in a separate shallow bowl, stirring with a whisk. Dredge steaks in breading mix. Dip in egg mixture; dredge again in breading mix.

2. Coat a large skillet with cooking spray. Add 1 tablespoon oil; place over medium-high heat until hot. Fry 2 steaks in hot oil 4 minutes on each side or until golden brown. Transfer steaks to a platter. Repeat procedure with remaining 1 tablespoon oil and remaining 2 steaks, reserving drippings in pan.

3. Combine remaining 1½ cups soy milk, cornstarch, salt, and pepper in a 2-cup glass measure, stirring with a whisk until smooth. Stir milk mixture into drippings in pan. Bring to a boil over medium-high heat; cook, stirring constantly, 1 minute or until thickened. Spoon gravy over steaks. Sprinkle evenly with parsley. **Yield: 4 servings (serving size: 1 steak, ⅓ cup gravy, and 1 teaspoon parsley).**

CALORIES 460; FAT 19.6g (sat 4.2g, mono 8.9g, poly 4.1g); PROTEIN 35.3g; CARB 34g; FIBER 2.3g; CHOL 170mg; IRON 4.8mg; SODIUM 538mg; CALC 55mg

Basic Breading Mix for Fried Foods:

Combine ½ cup brown rice flour, ½ cup cornmeal (such as Bob's Red Mill), 1 teaspoon dried parsley, ½ teaspoon fine sea salt, ½ teaspoon sugar, ½ teaspoon onion powder, ½ teaspoon garlic powder, ¼ teaspoon celery salt, ¼ teaspoon paprika, and ¼ teaspoon freshly ground black pepper in a small bowl, stirring with a whisk. **Yield: 1 cup.**

Nutritional analysis is for 1 cup of breading mix. CALORIES 602; FAT 3.8g (sat 0.6g, mono 1.1g, poly 1.4g); PROTEIN 12.1g; CARB 128.3g; FIBER 7.5g; CHOL 0mg; IRON 5.7mg; SODIUM 484mg; CALC 27mg

Old-Fashioned All-American Meat Loaf

☑ Dairy **free**
{Check for **Gluten**}

Cider vinegar and Worcestershire sauce add zing to the tomato topping on this homey loaf.

2 large egg whites
½ teaspoon salt, divided
½ teaspoon black pepper
1 pound extra-lean ground beef
½ cup finely chopped green bell pepper
½ cup finely chopped onion
1 (8-ounce) can no-salt-added tomato sauce, divided
1 (2-ounce) slice gluten-free bread, torn into 4 pieces
Cooking spray
1 tablespoon sugar
2 teaspoons cider vinegar
2 teaspoons Worcestershire sauce

1. Preheat oven to 350°.
2. Combine egg whites, ¼ teaspoon salt, and pepper in a large bowl, stirring with a whisk. Add beef, bell pepper, onion, and ½ cup tomato sauce to egg mixture. Place bread pieces in a food processor; process until fine crumbs form. Add crumbs to beef mixture, mixing with hands just until combined. Shape beef mixture into an 8 x 5-inch loaf. Place on a foil-lined baking sheet coated with cooking spray.
3. Combine remaining tomato sauce, remaining ¼ teaspoon salt, sugar, vinegar, and Worcestershire sauce in a small bowl, stirring with a spoon. Reserve 2 tablespoons tomato sauce mixture. Spoon remaining sauce mixture over top of loaf.
4. Bake at 350° for 45 minutes or until done. Remove from oven, and spoon reserved sauce over meat loaf. Let stand 10 minutes before cutting into 8 slices. **Yield: 4 servings (serving size: 2 slices).**

CALORIES 223; FAT 5.5g (sat 1.5g, mono 2g, poly 0.5g); PROTEIN 24.9g; CARB 17.5g; FIBER 1.9g; CHOL 60mg; IRON 2.7mg; SODIUM 471mg; CALC 12mg

Herbes de Provence–Crusted Lamb Chops

☑ Dairy **free**

The Dijon mustard and dried herbs rub also tastes great on chicken thighs or beef fillets. Herbes de Provence is a combination of several dried herbs—including lavender, thyme, rosemary, and basil—that evokes flavors from the south of France.

2 tablespoons Dijon mustard
1 tablespoon dried herbes de Provence
½ teaspoon kosher salt
¼ teaspoon freshly ground black pepper
1 garlic clove, minced
8 (4-ounce) lamb loin chops, trimmed
Cooking spray

1. Preheat grill to medium-high heat.

2. Combine first 5 ingredients; rub evenly over both sides of lamb.

3. Place lamb on grill rack coated with cooking spray; grill 4 minutes on each side or until desired degree of doneness.

Yield: 4 servings (serving size: 2 lamb chops).

CALORIES 220; FAT 10g (sat 3.4g, mono 4.3g, poly 0.8g); PROTEIN 29.2g; CARB 1.7g; FIBER 0.6g; CHOL 90mg; IRON 2.6mg; SODIUM 505mg; CALC 44mg

Grilled Red Potatoes with Mint:

Preheat grill to medium-high heat. Toss 1½ pounds small red potatoes with 1 teaspoon kosher salt and 2 teaspoons olive oil. Place potatoes ¼ inch apart on grill rack coated with cooking spray. Grill 15 minutes; turn over with tongs. Grill 15 minutes or until done. Cool slightly. Cut potatoes in half; toss with ⅓ cup thinly sliced mint leaves. **Yield: 4 servings.**

CALORIES 142; FAT 2.5g (sat 0.4g, mono 1.7g, poly 0.4g); PROTEIN 3.5g; CARB 27.7g; FIBER 3.4g; CHOL 0mg; IRON 2.2mg; SODIUM 372mg; CALC 32mg

Pork Tenderloin with Smoky Espresso Rub

☑ Dairy **free**

Turn up the wow factor as pork tenderloin gets dressed up with the palate-pleasing tastes of smoky and sweet.

- 1 tablespoon brown sugar
- 1½ teaspoons Spanish smoked paprika
- 1 teaspoon garlic powder
- 1 teaspoon instant espresso granules or 2 teaspoons instant coffee granules
- ½ teaspoon salt
- ½ teaspoon onion powder
- ½ teaspoon coarsely ground black pepper
- 1 (1-pound) pork tenderloin, trimmed
- Cooking spray
- 1 teaspoon olive oil
- ½ cup water

1. Preheat oven to 425°.

2. Combine first 7 ingredients. Rub sugar mixture over pork. Cover and let stand 15 minutes.

3. Heat a large ovenproof skillet over medium-high heat. Coat pan with cooking spray. Heat oil in pan. Add pork; cook 2 minutes on each side or until browned. Bake at 425° for 20 minutes or until a thermometer registers 160° (slightly pink).

4. Remove pork from pan, reserving drippings in pan. Cover pork and let stand 5 minutes. Stir ½ cup water into drippings, scraping pan to loosen browned bits. Drizzle sauce over pork.

Yield: 4 servings (serving size: 3 ounces pork and 4 teaspoons sauce).

CALORIES 151; FAT 3.9g (sat 1g, mono 1.9g, poly 0.6g); PROTEIN 24.1g; CARB 3.7g; FIBER 0.5g; CHOL 74mg; IRON 1.4mg; SODIUM 352mg; CALC 12mg

Sweet and Sour Pork

1½ pounds pork tenderloin, cut into 1-inch pieces
2 teaspoons grated peeled fresh ginger
2 garlic cloves, minced
½ teaspoon crushed red pepper, divided
1 (20-ounce) can pineapple chunks in juice, undrained
9 tablespoons fat-free, lower-sodium chicken broth, divided
¼ cup ketchup
¼ cup sugar
3 tablespoons cider vinegar
3 tablespoons lower-sodium soy sauce
1 tablespoon cornstarch
2 tablespoons peanut oil
1 medium onion, cut into 1-inch pieces
1 green bell pepper, cut into 1-inch pieces (about 1 cup)
1 red bell pepper, cut into 1-inch pieces (about 1 cup)
1 (8-ounce) can sliced water chestnuts, drained
3 cups hot cooked brown or white rice
1 green onion, cut diagonally into thin slices (optional)

1. Combine first 3 ingredients and ¼ teaspoon crushed red pepper in a bowl. Set aside.

2. Drain pineapple, reserving ¼ cup juice. Combine reserved juice, 6 tablespoons stock, ketchup, next 3 ingredients, and remaining ¼ teaspoon crushed red pepper in a small bowl, stirring until sugar dissolves. Combine cornstarch and remaining stock in another small bowl.

3. Heat oil in a large nonstick skillet over medium-high heat. Stir-fry pork mixture in hot oil 5 minutes or until pork is done. Remove pork from pan; keep warm. Add onion, bell peppers, and water chestnuts to pan; stir-fry 3 minutes or until crisp-tender. Add ketchup mixture. Bring to a boil; stir in cornstarch mixture, pineapple chunks, and pork mixture with any accumulated juices. Cook 2 minutes or until sauce thickens. Serve immediately over rice. Garnish with green onion slices, if desired. **Yield: 6 servings (serving size: 1 cup pork and ½ cup rice).**

CALORIES 405; FAT 8g (sat 1.8g, mono 3.3g, poly 2.2g); PROTEIN 27.8g; CARB 54.1g; FIBER 4.1g; CHOL 74mg; IRON 2.5mg; SODIUM 433mg; CALC 31mg

I made the Sweet and Sour Pork with my mother and sister. We had all given up this dish when eating out—the batter and super sweet sauce didn't fit my diet plan even before I had to become gluten free. This was a tasty and much lighter alternative. We loved the flavors of pineapple and peppers with the crunch of the water chestnuts.

—Sherl Taylor

Walnut-Crusted Pork Chops with Autumn Vegetable Wild Rice

☑ Dairy **free**
{Check for **Gluten**}

Apples, mushrooms, and Swiss chard make a nice contrast to the texture of wild rice.

4 (8-ounce) bone-in center-cut pork chops, trimmed
1½ teaspoons Worcestershire sauce
¾ teaspoon kosher salt
½ teaspoon dried rubbed sage
¼ teaspoon freshly ground black pepper
⅓ cup walnuts, finely ground
1 bacon slice
¼ cup fat-free, lower-sodium chicken broth
Cooking spray
1 cup finely chopped onion
½ cup diced carrot
2 teaspoons diced seeded jalapeño pepper
1 garlic clove, minced
1½ cups chopped Swiss chard
1 cup sliced cremini mushrooms
1 cup chopped peeled Granny Smith apple
2 cups cooked wild rice
½ cup fat-free, lower-sodium chicken broth
¼ cup chopped fresh flat-leaf parsley

1. Place pork in a shallow dish; drizzle evenly with Worcestershire sauce. Combine salt, sage, and black pepper in a small bowl. Reserve ¾ teaspoon salt mixture. Add walnuts to remaining salt mixture; toss well. Press walnut mixture onto both sides of pork. Cover and refrigerate 30 minutes.

2. Cook bacon slice in a large nonstick skillet over medium heat until crisp. Remove bacon from pan; crumble. Add pork to drippings in pan; cook 1½ minutes on each side or until lightly browned. Add ¼ cup chicken broth to pan. Cover, reduce heat, and cook 6 minutes or until desired degree of doneness. Remove pork from pan.

3. Heat a large saucepan over medium heat. Coat pan with cooking spray. Add onion and next 3 ingredients to pan; cover and cook 5 minutes or until onion is tender. Stir in reserved ¾ teaspoon salt mixture, chard, mushrooms, and apple. Cover and cook 5 minutes or until carrot is tender. Stir in rice and ½ cup broth. Bring to a simmer; cook, uncovered, 5 minutes or until liquid is absorbed. Stir in bacon. Place 1 cup rice mixture on each of 4 plates; top each serving with 1 pork chop. Drizzle each serving with pan drippings, and sprinkle each with 1 tablespoon parsley. **Yield: 4 servings.**

CALORIES 379; FAT 14.7g (sat 3.5g, mono 4.4g, poly 5.5g); PROTEIN 29.1g; CARB 34.6g; FIBER 5g; CHOL 69mg; IRON 2.6mg; SODIUM 600mg; CALC 65mg

Cooking Tip

Get a head start by assembling the stuffed pork chops the night before. Sprinkle them with the fennel seed mixture just before grilling.

Grilled Plum and Prosciutto–Stuffed Pork Chops

The balsamic vinegar and sweet molasses glaze balances out the spicy flavor of the rub on the pork.

4 pitted dried plums, halved
2 very thin slices prosciutto (about ¾ ounce), halved
½ teaspoon crushed fennel seeds
½ teaspoon chopped fresh sage
½ teaspoon chopped fresh rosemary
½ teaspoon paprika
¼ teaspoon kosher salt
¼ teaspoon crushed red pepper
¼ teaspoon freshly ground black pepper
4 (4-ounce) boneless center-cut loin pork chops (about ¾ inch thick)
Cooking spray
2 teaspoons balsamic vinegar
2 teaspoons molasses

1. Preheat grill to medium-high heat.
2. Soak plum halves in boiling water 5 minutes. Drain well.
3. Wrap 2 plum halves in each prosciutto piece.
4. Combine fennel seeds and next 6 ingredients in a small bowl.
5. Cut a horizontal slit through thickest portion of each pork chop to form a pocket. Stuff 1 prosciutto wrap into each pocket. Sprinkle pork chops with fennel seed mixture. Place pork chops on grill rack coated with cooking spray; grill 5 minutes on each side or until desired degree of doneness. Combine vinegar and molasses; brush over pork chops. **Yield: 4 servings (serving size: 1 chop).**

CALORIES 205; FAT 7.2g (sat 2.6g, mono 2.9g, poly 0.5g); PROTEIN 25.7g; CARB 8.5g; FIBER 0.9g; CHOL 70mg; IRON 1.3mg; SODIUM 270mg; CALC 42mg

Hominy Sauté:

Melt 2 teaspoons butter in a large nonstick skillet. Add ½ cup chopped onion and 2 minced garlic cloves; sauté 2 minutes or until tender. Add 1 (15.5-ounce) can drained white hominy, ¼ cup chopped green onions, ¼ teaspoon salt, and ¼ teaspoon freshly ground black pepper. Cook 2 minutes or until thoroughly heated. **Yield: 4 servings.**

CALORIES 81; FAT 2.6g (sat 1.3g, mono 0.7g, poly 0.4g); PROTEIN 1.4g; CARB 13.1g; FIBER 2.4g; CHOL 5mg; IRON 0.6mg; SODIUM 311mg; CALC 21mg

Spicy Herb-Rubbed Grilled Chicken

☑ Dairy **free**

Place zucchini and red bell peppers next to the chicken on the grill for an easy and colorful side.

1 teaspoon onion powder
1 teaspoon garlic powder
1 teaspoon dried oregano
½ teaspoon salt
½ teaspoon cayenne pepper
½ teaspoon freshly ground black
   pepper
4 (6-ounce) chicken breast
   halves
Cooking spray

1. Preheat grill to medium-high heat.
2. Combine first 6 ingredients in a small bowl. Sprinkle spice mixture evenly over both sides of chicken, pressing lightly to adhere. Place chicken on grill rack coated with cooking spray; grill 6 minutes on each side or until done. **Yield: 4 servings (serving size: 1 chicken breast half).**

CALORIES 194; FAT 2.2g (sat 0.6g, mono 0.5g, poly 0.5g); PROTEIN 39.5g; CARB 1.5g; FIBER 0.3g; CHOL 99mg; IRON 1.4mg; SODIUM 406mg; CALC 27mg

Cooking Tip

Commercial rubs may contain gluten, so keep this simple but versatile six-ingredient rub in your pantry. It quickly turns ordinary steak, chicken, or fish fillets into a tasty entrée. Vary the main herb, oregano, to suit your taste—the same amount of dried basil or thyme is just as delicious. Store it in an airtight container to maintain freshness.

Lemon-Chardonnay Grilled Chicken

☑ Dairy **free**

Reserving a portion of the marinade to spoon on after cooking is the key to giving this chicken extra flavor. You can serve this with a quick side of steamed broccoli and gluten-free penne.

1 tablespoon grated lemon rind
2 tablespoons fresh lemon juice
2 tablespoons chardonnay or other dry white wine
2 tablespoons extra-virgin olive oil
1 tablespoon fresh oregano leaves
½ teaspoon dried dill
¼ teaspoon crushed red pepper
2 medium garlic cloves, minced
4 (6-ounce) skinless, boneless chicken breast halves
Cooking spray
¼ teaspoon salt

1. Combine first 8 ingredients in a medium bowl, stirring with a whisk. Reserve 2 tablespoons marinade. Add chicken to remaining marinade in bowl, turning to coat. Cover and marinate in refrigerator 15 minutes, turning chicken occasionally.

2. Heat a large nonstick grill pan over medium-high heat. Coat pan with cooking spray. Remove chicken from bowl, discarding marinade. Add chicken to pan; cook 6 minutes on each side or until done. Place chicken on a serving platter.

3. Stir salt into reserved marinade; spoon evenly over chicken.

Yield: 4 servings (serving size: 1 chicken breast half).

CALORIES 213; FAT 4.6g (sat 0.9g, mono 2.3g, poly 0.7g); PROTEIN 39.4g; CARB 0.6g; FIBER 0.1g; CHOL 99mg; IRON 1.3mg; SODIUM 256mg; CALC 23mg

Chicken Tacos with Mango-Avocado Salsa

☑ Dairy **free**

Your family will thank you when these tacos hit the table. We left the seeds in the jalapeño for a spicy kick; omit them if you prefer a mild salsa. For a tip on warming gluten-free tortillas, see page 211.

1 teaspoon garlic powder
1 teaspoon paprika
½ teaspoon onion powder
¼ teaspoon ground red pepper
¾ teaspoon salt, divided
4 (6-ounce) skinless, boneless chicken breast halves
1½ teaspoons olive oil
½ cup diced peeled mango
½ cup diced peeled avocado
½ cup chopped tomato
⅓ cup chopped onion
2 tablespoons chopped fresh cilantro
2 tablespoons fresh lime juice
1 tablespoon minced jalapeño pepper
4 (8-inch) brown rice tortillas (such as Food for Life)

1. Heat a nonstick skillet over medium-high heat. Combine first 4 ingredients; stir in ½ teaspoon salt. Rub over chicken. Add oil to pan; swirl to coat. Add chicken; cook 4 minutes on each side or until done. Remove chicken from pan; let stand 5 minutes. Cut into ¼-inch-thick slices.

2. While chicken cooks, combine mango and next 6 ingredients; stir in remaining ¼ teaspoon salt.

3. Warm tortillas; top evenly with chicken and salsa. **Yield: 4 servings (serving size: 1 tortilla, 1 chicken breast half, and ½ cup salsa).**

CALORIES 392; FAT 9.3g (sat 1.2g, mono 4.2g, poly 2.3g); PROTEIN 42.4g; CARB 33.1g; FIBER 4.5g; CHOL 99mg; IRON 2.1mg; SODIUM 711mg; CALC 33mg

Chicken Enchiladas

{Check for **Gluten**}

1½ pounds skinless, boneless chicken breast halves
2 teaspoons olive oil
2 cups chopped onion
½ cup water
1 tablespoon chili powder
1½ teaspoons ground cumin
½ teaspoon salt
½ teaspoon black pepper
1 (14.5-ounce) can no-salt-added diced tomatoes, undrained
1 (4-ounce) can chopped green chiles, drained
1 (8-ounce) tub light cream cheese
Cooking spray
12 (6-inch) corn tortillas
1 cup (4 ounces) shredded reduced-fat sharp cheddar cheese
Chopped green onions (optional)
Chopped fresh cilantro (optional)

1. Preheat oven to 350°.

2. Place chicken in a medium saucepan and cover with water. Bring to a boil; cover, reduce heat, and simmer 15 minutes or until tender. Drain chicken, and cool slightly. Shred chicken with 2 forks, and place in a large bowl.

3. Heat oil in a large nonstick skillet over medium-high heat. Add onion; sauté 5 minutes or until tender. Add half of onion to chicken. Place remaining half of onion, ½ cup water, and next 6 ingredients in a blender; process until smooth.

4. Add ½ cup tomato mixture and cream cheese to chicken mixture. Spread ½ cup tomato mixture in bottom of a 13 x 9–inch baking dish coated with cooking spray; return remaining tomato mixture to pan. Heat over low heat until warm; keep warm.

5. Working with 1 tortilla at a time, dip tortilla in warm sauce in pan, coating both sides. Place on a plate; spoon 3 tablespoons chicken filling onto each tortilla; roll up, and place in dish. Spoon remaining sauce over enchiladas in dish. Sprinkle enchiladas with cheddar cheese.

6. Bake, uncovered, at 350° for 30 minutes or until thoroughly heated. Garnish with green onions and cilantro, if desired. **Yield: 6 servings (serving size: 2 enchiladas).**

CALORIES 449; FAT 14.8g (sat 6.6g, mono 4.7g, poly 1.6g); PROTEIN 37.7g; CARB 40.4g; FIBER 3.9g; CHOL 97mg; IRON 1.6mg; SODIUM 767; CALC 428mg

These enchiladas were relatively simple to prepare,

and the recipe called for ingredients that I would ordinarily already have in my kitchen, which is great! I might replace the can of mild chili peppers with one or two fresh jalapeño peppers for a bit more spice.

—*Peggy Christoffer*

Grilled Tandoori Chicken

Named for "tandoor," the Indian clay oven it's traditionally cooked in, this dish is tender and tasty. Serve with rice and zucchini.

  2 teaspoons canola oil
  4 teaspoons Hungarian sweet paprika
  2 teaspoons ground cumin, divided
  2 teaspoons ground coriander, divided
  2 teaspoons garam masala
  1 teaspoon ground turmeric
  1 teaspoon ground red pepper
  2 cups coarsely chopped onion
  ½ cup coarsely chopped peeled fresh ginger
  2 teaspoons finely chopped seeded serrano chile
  8 garlic cloves, crushed
2½ cups plain low-fat yogurt, divided
  ¼ cup fresh lemon juice, divided
  2 teaspoons salt, divided
 16 skinless, boneless chicken thighs (about 3 pounds)
    Cooking spray

1. Heat oil in a small nonstick skillet over medium-high heat. Add paprika, 1½ teaspoons cumin, 1½ teaspoons coriander, garam masala, turmeric, and red pepper to pan; cook 2 minutes or until fragrant, stirring constantly. Remove from pan; cool.

2. Place onion and next 3 ingredients in a food processor; process until smooth. Add spice mixture, ½ cup yogurt, 2 tablespoons juice, and 1¾ teaspoons salt to onion mixture; process until smooth. Transfer mixture to a large heavy-duty zip-top plastic bag. Cut 3 shallow slits in each chicken thigh. Add chicken to bag, and seal. Toss to coat. Marinate in refrigerator 8 hours or overnight, turning occasionally.

3. Preheat grill to medium-high heat.

4. Combine remaining 2 cups yogurt, remaining 2 tablespoons juice, remaining ½ teaspoon cumin, remaining ½ teaspoon coriander, and remaining ¼ teaspoon salt in a bowl, stirring well. Cover and chill.

5. Remove chicken from bag; discard marinade. Place chicken on grill rack coated with cooking spray. Grill 7 minutes on each side or until done. Serve with yogurt mixture. **Yield: 8 servings (serving size: 2 chicken thighs and about ¼ cup yogurt mixture).**

CALORIES 256; FAT 8.1g (sat 2.3g, mono 2.7g, poly 1.8g); PROTEIN 32.2g; CARB 12.7g; FIBER 1.7g; CHOL 119mg; IRON 2.2mg; SODIUM 767mg; CALC 181mg

Parmesan-Almond Chicken Cutlets

{Check for **Gluten**}

1 cup finely ground almond meal
¼ cup (1 ounce) grated fresh Parmesan cheese
½ teaspoon freshly ground black pepper
¼ teaspoon salt
½ cup water
8 chicken cutlets (about 2 pounds)
2 tablespoons olive oil, divided
Cooking spray
½ cup fat-free, lower-sodium chicken broth
3 tablespoons fresh lemon juice
2 tablespoons drained capers
¼ cup chopped fresh flat-leaf parsley
1 lemon, cut into 8 wedges (optional)

1. Combine first 4 ingredients in a shallow bowl. Place ½ cup water in another shallow bowl. Dip chicken in water, shaking off excess; dredge in almond meal mixture.

2. Heat a large nonstick skillet over medium-high heat. Add 1 tablespoon oil to pan. Place 4 cutlets in hot oil; reduce heat to medium, and cook 5 minutes. Coat cutlets with cooking spray. Turn cutlets over; cook 3 minutes or until done. Remove cutlets from pan, and keep warm. Repeat procedure with remaining oil and chicken.

3. Increase heat to medium-high. Stir in broth and lemon juice, scraping pan to loosen browned bits. Add capers, and cook 1 to 2 minutes or until sauce is syrupy and reduced by half. Pour sauce over chicken cutlets; sprinkle with parsley. Serve with lemon wedges, if desired. **Yield: 4 servings (serving size: 2 cutlets and 2 tablespoons sauce).**

CALORIES 462; FAT 21.9g (sat 3.4g, mono 13g, poly 4.1g); PROTEIN 59.6g; CARB 6.5g; FIBER 2.6g; CHOL 136mg; IRON 2.9mg; SODIUM 583mg; CALC 138mg

Cooking Tip

Almond meal is simply skinless, blanched almonds that have been finely ground, which means it's packed with healthy fats and protein. It also lends a rich flavor to these cutlets.

Roast Turkey with Simple Turkey Gravy

☑ Dairy **free**
{Check for **Gluten**}

You can use ¼ cup fat-free, lower-sodium chicken broth in place of the turkey drippings, if you'd like.

1 (12-pound) fresh or frozen turkey, thawed
½ cup spicy brown mustard
¼ cup packed chopped fresh sage leaves
½ teaspoon freshly ground black pepper
2 garlic cloves, minced
4 cups fat-free, lower-sodium chicken broth, divided
2 tablespoons gluten-free all-purpose flour (such as Bob's Red Mill)
½ teaspoon onion powder
¼ teaspoon salt
¼ teaspoon poultry seasoning
¼ teaspoon freshly ground black pepper

1. Preheat oven to 450°.

2. Remove and discard giblets and neck from turkey. Rinse turkey with cold running water, and pat dry. Trim excess fat. Starting at neck cavity, loosen skin from breast and drumsticks by inserting fingers, gently pushing between skin and meat. Combine mustard, sage, black pepper, and garlic. Rub mustard mixture under loosened skin over flesh. Lift wing tips up and over back; tuck under turkey. Secure legs with kitchen twine.

3. Place turkey, breast side up, in a shallow roasting pan. Pour 2 cups broth over turkey. Place turkey in oven; reduce oven temperature to 325°.

4. Bake, uncovered, at 325° for 2 hours and 20 minutes or until a thermometer inserted in thickest part of thigh registers 165°, basting turkey frequently with pan juices. Transfer turkey to a large serving platter, reserving ¼ cup drippings. Loosely cover turkey with foil, and let stand 25 minutes.

5. Combine reserved drippings, flour, and next 4 ingredients in a medium saucepan, stirring with a whisk until smooth. Gradually stir in remaining 2 cups broth. Bring to a boil over medium-high heat, stirring constantly with a whisk. Reduce heat, and simmer 2 minutes or until gravy thickens, stirring occasionally. Remove from heat.

6. Discard turkey skin; carve. Serve turkey with gravy. **Yield: 14 servings (serving size: about 5 ounces turkey and 2 table-spoons gravy).**

CALORIES 327; FAT 7.5g (sat 2.5g, mono 1.6g, poly 2.2g); PROTEIN 57.4g; CARB 1.4g; FIBER 0.2g; CHOL 169mg; IRON 3.9mg; SODIUM 406mg; CALC 42mg

Nam Sod

 Dairy **free**

Roll up bites of this spicy Thai turkey salad in crunchy cabbage leaves for a super-flavorful light meal or appetizer. Increase the sambal oelek to 2 teaspoons if you like a little more heat.

Cooking spray
1 pound ground turkey breast
½ cup thin vertical slices red onion
⅓ cup finely chopped green onions
3 tablespoons fresh lime juice
1½ tablespoons fish sauce (such as Thai Kitchen)
1 tablespoon minced peeled fresh ginger
1 teaspoon chile paste with garlic (such as sambal oelek)
2 tablespoons dry-roasted peanuts
½ small head green or Napa (Chinese) cabbage, separated into leaves

1. Heat a large nonstick skillet over medium-high heat. Coat pan with cooking spray. Add turkey to pan; cook 5 minutes or until done, stirring to crumble. Remove turkey from pan; set aside to cool.

2. Combine onion slices and next 5 ingredients in a medium bowl. Let stand 10 minutes. Stir turkey into onion mixture; sprinkle with peanuts.

3. Serve turkey mixture in cabbage leaves. **Yield: 4 servings (serving size: ¾ cup turkey filling and 3 cabbage leaves).**

CALORIES 188; FAT 4.1g (sat 0.9g, mono 1.2g, poly 0.8g); PROTEIN 29.4g; CARB 9.7g; FIBER 3.1g; CHOL 46mg; IRON 1.5mg; SODIUM 648mg; CALC 53mg

Smoky Sausage and Peppers on Cheddary Brown Rice Farina

{Check for **Gluten**}

2¼ cups water, divided
1½ cups fat-free milk
½ teaspoon salt
½ teaspoon dried thyme
1 cup uncooked brown rice farina
2 teaspoons canola oil, divided
4 ounces (½-inch) cubed smoked turkey sausage
1 cup chopped onion
1 cup chopped red bell pepper
2 medium garlic cloves, minced
⅛ teaspoon crushed red pepper
¾ cup (3 ounces) shredded reduced-fat sharp cheddar cheese

1. Bring 2 cups water, milk, salt, and thyme to a boil in a large saucepan. Gradually stir in farina; reduce heat, and simmer, uncovered, 4 minutes, stirring occasionally.

2. While farina cooks, heat 1 teaspoon oil in a large nonstick skillet over medium-high heat. Add sausage, and cook 3 minutes or until browned, stirring frequently. Remove from pan; set aside, and keep warm. Add remaining 1 teaspoon oil to pan; add onion and bell pepper. Sauté 5 minutes or until onion begins to brown. Stir in garlic and crushed red pepper; sauté 15 seconds. Remove from heat. Stir in sausage and remaining ¼ cup water, scraping pan to loosen browned bits.

3. Spoon farina evenly onto each of 4 plates. Sprinkle evenly with cheese. Spoon sausage mixture evenly over cheese.

Yield: 4 servings (serving size: ¾ cup farina, 3 tablespoons cheese, and ½ cup sausage topping).

CALORIES 339; FAT 11g (sat 3.7g, mono 4g, poly 1.6g); PROTEIN 16.5g; CARB 44.8g; FIBER 3.5g; CHOL 36mg; IRON 1.6mg; SODIUM 781mg; CALC 443mg

Pizzas & Pastas

Pepperoni Pizza

{Check for **Gluten**}

Cooking spray

2 cups thinly sliced cremini mushrooms (about 4 ounces)

1 (16-ounce) package frozen fresh gluten-free pizza crust dough (such as Gillian's), thawed

1 tablespoon cornmeal (such as Bob's Red Mill)

2 teaspoons olive oil

1⅓ cups Basic Pizza Sauce (page 167) or bottled gluten-free pizza sauce

1½ cups (6 ounces) shredded part-skim mozzarella cheese

2 tablespoons grated fresh Parmesan cheese

{ 2 ounces sliced turkey pepperoni

1. Place 1 oven rack in the middle position. Place another rack in the lowest position. Preheat oven to 500°.

2. Heat a large nonstick skillet over medium-high heat. Coat pan with cooking spray. Add sliced mushrooms to pan, and sauté 5 minutes or until moisture evaporates.

3. Place dough on a rimless baking sheet sprinkled with 1 tablespoon cornmeal. Press dough into a 12-inch circle (about ¼ inch thick). Crimp edges of dough with fingers to form a ½-inch border. Brush oil over dough. Bake on lowest oven rack at 500° for 8 minutes. Remove from oven.

4. Spread Basic Pizza Sauce in an even layer over crust to the border. Top sauce with mushrooms. Sprinkle mushrooms evenly with mozzarella and Parmesan. Arrange pepperoni in an even layer on top of cheese. Bake on middle rack an additional 10 minutes or until crust is golden brown and cheese melts. Cut into 12 wedges. **Yield: 6 servings (serving size: 2 wedges).**

CALORIES 350; FAT 12.8g (sat 4.4g, mono 3g, poly 0.6g); PROTEIN 17.7g; CARB 42.9g; FIBER 1.9g; CHOL 28mg; IRON 3.2mg; SODIUM 782mg; CALC 274mg

Pizza Margherita

Because this classic Neapolitan-style pizza is so simple, it depends on quality ingredients. Use the best fresh mozzarella and basil you can find.

½ (24-ounce) package frozen prebaked gluten-free pizza crusts, thawed

½ cup Basic Pizza Sauce or bottled gluten-free pizza sauce

5 ounces fresh mozzarella cheese, thinly sliced

⅓ cup torn fresh basil leaves

1. Preheat oven to 450°.

2. Place pizza crust on a baking sheet. Spread Basic Pizza Sauce evenly over crust. Arrange cheese slices over sauce. Place on bottom rack of oven.

3. Bake at 450° for 12 minutes. Remove from oven, and sprinkle with basil. Cut into 10 wedges. Serve immediately. **Yield: 5 servings (serving size: 2 wedges).**

CALORIES 238; FAT 9g (sat 4g, mono 1g, poly 3.2g); PROTEIN 10.2g; CARB 31.9g; FIBER 4.4g; CHOL 29mg; IRON 1.9mg; SODIUM 376mg; CALC 68mg

Basic Pizza Sauce:

Heat a large saucepan over medium-high heat. Coat pan with cooking spray. Add ¼ cup finely chopped onion to pan; sauté 3 minutes or until tender. Add 1 minced garlic clove to pan; sauté 30 seconds. Stir in ¼ cup white wine; cook 30 seconds. Add 2 tablespoons tomato paste, 1 teaspoon dried oregano, ⅛ teaspoon freshly ground black pepper, and 1 (14.5-ounce) can undrained crushed tomatoes. Reduce heat, and simmer 20 minutes or until thick. Remove from heat; stir in 1 tablespoon chopped fresh basil and ½ teaspoon balsamic vinegar. Cool. **Yield: 1⅓ cups.**

Nutritional analysis is for 1⅓ cups Basic Pizza Sauce. CALORIES 202; FAT 0.3g (sat 0.1g, mono 0g, poly 0.1g); PROTEIN 9.6g; CARB 42g; FIBER 9.9g; CHOL 0mg; IRON 7.1mg; SODIUM 955mg; CALC 197mg

Spicy Pizza Sauce variation: Add ½ teaspoon crushed red pepper with the oregano and black pepper; omit basil. **Yield: 1⅓ cups.**

Nutritional analysis is for 1⅓ cups Spicy Pizza Sauce. CALORIES 206; FAT 0.4g (sat 0.1g, mono 0.1g, poly 0.2g); PROTEIN 9.6g; CARB 42.6g; FIBER 10.3g; CHOL 0mg; IRON 7.3mg; SODIUM 953mg; CALC 199mg

"The Works" Pizza

Use the basic pizza crust in this recipe in place of store-bought versions in other recipes.

Topping:
- 1 teaspoon olive oil
- ¼ pound bulk sausage
- 1 cup chopped red bell pepper (about 1 small)
- 1 cup sliced button mushrooms
- ½ cup finely chopped onion (about 1 small)
- 1 small garlic clove, minced
- ¼ cup sliced, drained ripe olives

Crust:
- 1 package active dry yeast (about 2¼ teaspoons)
- 2½ teaspoons sugar, divided
- 1 cup warm soy milk or 2% reduced-fat milk (100° to 110°)
- 4.4 ounces brown rice flour (about 1 cup), divided
- ½ cup cornstarch
- 2 teaspoons xanthan gum
- 1 teaspoon dried Italian seasoning
- ½ teaspoon fine sea salt
- 4 teaspoons olive oil, divided
- 2 teaspoons cider vinegar
- Cooking spray

Remaining Ingredients:
- ¾ cup bottled gluten-free pizza sauce
- 1½ cups (6 ounces) shredded part-skim mozzarella cheese

1. Preheat oven to 450°.

2. To prepare topping, heat 1 teaspoon olive oil in a heavy medium skillet over medium heat. Cook sausage in hot oil 5 minutes or until browned; stir to crumble. Add bell pepper, mushrooms, and onion; cook 4 minutes or until vegetables are tender, stirring occasionally. Add garlic; sauté 1 minute. Stir in olives; drain sausage mixture on paper towels.

3. To prepare crust, dissolve yeast and ½ teaspoon sugar in warm soy milk in a small bowl; let stand 5 minutes.

4. Weigh or lightly spoon 3.3 ounces brown rice flour (¾ cup) into dry measuring cups; level with a knife. Place brown rice flour, remaining 2 teaspoons sugar, cornstarch, and next 3 ingredients in a food processor. With processor on, pour yeast mixture, 1 tablespoon olive oil, and vinegar through food chute; process 30 seconds, adding 2 tablespoons brown rice flour, 1 tablespoon at a time if necessary, until mixture forms a ball.

5. Coat a 12-inch pizza pan with cooking spray. Place dough on pan; dust with remaining 2 tablespoons brown rice flour to prevent sticking to fingers. Press dough onto pan; crimp edges of dough with fingers to form a rim. Place on bottom rack of oven.

6. Bake at 450° for 10 minutes. Remove from oven, and brush edges of crust with remaining 1 teaspoon olive oil. Spread pizza sauce evenly over crust. Top with sausage mixture and cheese. Place on middle rack of oven. Bake at 450° for 15 minutes. Cool pizza in pan on a wire rack 5 minutes. Cut into 6 wedges. **Yield: 6 servings (serving size: 1 wedge).**

CALORIES 359; FAT 16g (sat 5.4g, mono 7.5g, poly 1.9g); PROTEIN 14.5g; CARB 39.3g; FIBER 4.2g; CHOL 32mg; IRON 2mg; SODIUM 622mg; CALC 264mg

Pear and Prosciutto Pizza

Pit peppery arugula against a base of creamy, sweet caramelized onions. Also appearing: prudent amounts of salty prosciutto, cheese, and walnuts.

2 teaspoons olive oil
2 cups vertically sliced sweet onion
½ (24-ounce) package frozen prebaked gluten-free pizza crusts, thawed
½ cup (2 ounces) shredded provolone cheese
1 medium pear, thinly sliced
2 ounces thinly sliced prosciutto, cut into thin strips
Dash of freshly ground black pepper
2 tablespoons chopped walnuts, toasted
1½ cups baby arugula leaves
1 teaspoon sherry vinegar

1. Preheat oven to 450°.

2. Heat oil in a large nonstick skillet over medium-high heat. Add onion to pan; cover and cook 3 minutes. Uncover and cook 10 minutes or until golden brown, stirring frequently. Top pizza crust with onion mixture; sprinkle with cheese. Layer pear and prosciutto over cheese; sprinkle with pepper. Place on middle rack of oven.

3. Bake at 450° for 12 minutes or until cheese melts. Sprinkle with walnuts.

4. Place arugula in a medium bowl just before serving. Drizzle vinegar over arugula; toss gently to coat. Top pizza with arugula mixture; cut into 8 wedges. Serve immediately. **Yield: 4 servings (serving size: 2 wedges).**

CALORIES 363; FAT 13.2g (sat 3.5g, mono 4.1g, poly 5.4g); PROTEIN 15.5g; CARB 51.8g; FIBER 7.6g; CHOL 25mg; IRON 2.3mg; SODIUM 741mg; CALC 205mg

Broccoli-Cheese Calzones

A small amount of red pepper adds a touch of heat, but feel free to add more if your taste buds like it hot.

1 teaspoon olive oil
1 cup broccoli florets
1 cup sliced mushrooms
¼ teaspoon crushed red pepper
1 (16-ounce) package frozen fresh gluten-free pizza crust dough (such as Gillian's), thawed
¼ cup gluten-free all-purpose flour (such as Bob's Red Mill)
1 cup (4 ounces) shredded part-skim mozzarella cheese
Cooking spray
1 cup bottled gluten-free pizza sauce, warmed (optional)

1. Preheat oven to 375°.
2. Line a baking sheet with parchment paper. Set aside.
3. Heat a large nonstick skillet over medium-high heat. Add oil, swirling to coat pan. Add broccoli, mushrooms, and red pepper; sauté 5 minutes or until lightly browned and moisture evaporates. Remove from heat.
4. Cut dough into 4 equal portions. Roll 1 portion into a 6-inch circle on a work surface sprinkled with 1 tablespoon flour. Repeat procedure with remaining dough and flour.
5. Spoon ¼ cup vegetable filling into center of each circle; sprinkle each with ¼ cup cheese. Brush edges of dough with water; fold dough in half over filling, pressing firmly to seal.
6. Place calzones on prepared baking sheet; coat tops with cooking spray. Bake at 375° for 15 minutes or until crust is golden brown. Cool slightly, and serve with warm pizza sauce, if desired. **Yield: 4 servings (serving size: 1 calzone).**

CALORIES 388; FAT 13.3g (sat 1.7g, mono 2.8g, poly 1.7g); PROTEIN 15.4g; CARB 55g; FIBER 1.5g; CHOL 0mg; IRON 2.8mg; SODIUM 431mg; CALC 14mg

Beef Calzones variation: Replace the vegetable filling with a meaty version. Starting with step 3, cook ½ pound ground sirloin, ½ cup chopped onion, 1 teaspoon onion powder, 1 teaspoon garlic powder, 1 teaspoon dried Italian seasoning, and 2 minced garlic cloves in a large nonstick skillet over medium-high heat 5 minutes, stirring to crumble beef. Drain. Continue the recipe starting with step 4.

CALORIES 483; FAT 17.7g (sat 3.8g, mono 4.5g, poly 1.7g); PROTEIN 26.1g; CARB 56.8g; FIBER 1.4g; CHOL 37mg; IRON 4mg; SODIUM 465mg; CALC 22mg

Cooking Tip

There are a variety of gluten-free pastas available. Most are made of corn, rice, quinoa, or buckwheat. Since these pastas lack wheat, which acts as a binder in traditional pasta, they cook differently and can get mushy quickly if overcooked. Reference the package when cooking each variety because cook times and procedures for the best results vary.

Baked Vegetable Lasagna

Don't press out extra water from the tofu for this recipe; that way, the cheesy layer will remain moist and creamy. Serve with a green salad.

3 tablespoons olive oil, divided
½ cup chopped white onion
2 garlic cloves, minced
1 teaspoon kosher salt, divided
1 teaspoon sugar
¼ teaspoon freshly ground black pepper, divided
¼ teaspoon crushed red pepper
1 (28-ounce) can crushed tomatoes, undrained
½ cup chopped fresh basil
1 tablespoon chopped fresh oregano
1 cup ricotta cheese
½ cup (2 ounces) grated fresh Parmigiano-Reggiano cheese
1 (14-ounce) package water-packed firm tofu, drained
1 large egg, lightly beaten
½ cup thinly sliced green onions
3 cups finely chopped red bell pepper (about 2 medium)
2 medium zucchini, quartered lengthwise and thinly sliced
⅓ cup chopped fresh parsley
Cooking spray
12 cooked gluten-free lasagna noodles
¾ cup (3 ounces) shredded part-skim mozzarella cheese

1. Preheat oven to 375°.

2. Heat 2 tablespoons oil in a medium saucepan over medium-high heat. Add white onion; sauté 5 minutes or until tender. Add garlic; sauté 1 minute or until golden. Add ½ teaspoon salt, sugar, ⅛ teaspoon black pepper, crushed red pepper, and tomatoes. Cover, reduce heat to low, and simmer 15 minutes or until thoroughly heated. Remove from heat; stir in basil and oregano. Cool.

3. Combine ricotta, Parmigiano-Reggiano, tofu, egg, and ¼ teaspoon salt in a food processor; process 10 seconds or until blended. Stir in green onions. Set aside.

4. Heat remaining 1 tablespoon olive oil in a large nonstick skillet over medium-high heat. Add bell pepper, zucchini, and remaining ¼ teaspoon salt to pan; sauté 10 minutes or until vegetables are tender and liquid evaporates. Remove from heat; stir in parsley and remaining ⅛ teaspoon black pepper.

5. Spread ½ cup tomato mixture in bottom of a 13 x 9–inch baking dish coated with cooking spray; top with 3 noodles. Spread ¾ cup tomato mixture over noodles; top with 1 cup tofu mixture and 1 cup zucchini mixture. Repeat layers twice, ending with noodles. Spread remaining ¾ cup tomato mixture over top. Bake at 375° for 35 minutes or until bubbly; top with mozzarella cheese. Bake an additional 5 minutes or until cheese melts. Let stand 10 minutes. **Yield: 8 servings (serving size: 1 piece).**

CALORIES 428; FAT 18g (sat 6.1g, mono 7g, poly 3.5g); PROTEIN 22.2g; CARB 46.8g; FIBER 5.2g; CHOL 54mg; IRON 3.6mg; SODIUM 572mg; CALC 607mg

Spinach and Mushroom Lasagna

This spinach and mushroom lasagna is a delicious change of pace from traditional lasagna recipes. It is sure to become a family favorite.

9 uncooked gluten-free lasagna noodles
1 teaspoon olive oil
7 cups sliced mushrooms
3 cups sliced shiitake mushroom caps
½ teaspoon ground nutmeg
3 garlic cloves, minced
2 (15-ounce) containers part-skim ricotta cheese
2 (10-ounce) packages frozen chopped spinach, thawed, drained, and squeezed dry
6 tablespoons grated fresh Parmesan cheese, divided
1 teaspoon dried Italian seasoning
1 teaspoon freshly ground black pepper
3 large egg whites
1 (25.5-ounce) jar gluten-free marinara sauce
Cooking spray
3 cups (12 ounces) shredded part-skim mozzarella cheese, divided
Fresh oregano leaves (optional)

1. Cook lasagna noodles according to package directions, omitting salt and fat. Drain; set aside.

2. Heat oil in a nonstick skillet over medium heat. Add mushrooms; sauté 3 minutes. Add nutmeg and garlic; sauté 5 minutes. Set aside.

3. Combine ricotta, spinach, ¼ cup Parmesan cheese, Italian seasoning, pepper, and egg whites; set aside.

4. Preheat oven to 375°.

5. Spread ½ cup marinara sauce in bottom of a 13 x 9–inch baking dish coated with cooking spray. Arrange 3 lasagna noodles over sauce; top with half of ricotta cheese mixture, half of mushroom mixture, 1½ cups sauce, and 1 cup mozzarella cheese. Repeat layers, ending with noodles. Spread ½ cup sauce over noodles.

6. Cover and bake at 375° for 40 minutes. Uncover; sprinkle with remaining 1 cup mozzarella cheese and remaining 2 tablespoons Parmesan cheese; bake 10 minutes. Let stand 10 minutes before serving. Garnish with oregano leaves, if desired.

Yield: 9 servings (serving size: 1 piece).

CALORIES 430; FAT 17.1g (sat 10.1g, mono 2.8g, poly 0.5g); PROTEIN 30.4g; CARB 39.1g; FIBER 4.3g; CHOL 52mg; IRON 3mg; SODIUM 741mg; CALC 661mg

Linguine with Peppery Shrimp

A generous amount of black pepper brings some welcome heat to this pasta dish.

2 pounds large shrimp, peeled
and deveined
4 teaspoons kosher salt, divided
1½ teaspoons freshly ground
black pepper
Cooking spray
½ teaspoon grated lemon rind
3 tablespoons fresh lemon juice
1 tablespoon chopped fresh
thyme, divided
3 tablespoons butter
6 quarts water
8 ounces uncooked gluten-free
quinoa linguine (such as
Ancient Harvest)

1. Combine shrimp, ½ teaspoon salt, and pepper, tossing to coat shrimp. Heat a large nonstick skillet over medium-high heat. Coat pan with cooking spray. Add shrimp; sauté 4 minutes or until shrimp are done.

2. Combine rind and juice in a small saucepan over medium heat; add 2 teaspoons thyme. Bring to a boil; add butter, stirring constantly with a whisk until butter melts. Bring 6 quarts water to a boil; stir in 1 tablespoon salt. Add pasta; cook 10 minutes or until al dente. Drain, reserving 2 tablespoons pasta water. Add shrimp, butter mixture, reserved pasta water, and remaining ½ teaspoon salt to pasta, tossing to coat. Sprinkle with remaining 1 teaspoon thyme. **Yield: 6 servings (serving size: about 1⅓ cups).**

CALORIES 350; FAT 9.1g (sat 4.1g, mono 2.5g, poly 1.2g); PROTEIN 33.5g; CARB 32.5g; FIBER 2.9g; CHOL 245mg; IRON 4.8mg; SODIUM 747mg; CALC 84mg

Three-Cheese Baked Penne

Since gluten-free pasta can clump and stick together if it stands for a while, be sure to cook it to al dente (since it'll cook a bit more while it bakes), and have it ready just in time to toss with the sauce.

2 teaspoons olive oil
1½ cups finely chopped onion (about 1 medium)
1 (12-ounce) package gluten-free brown rice penne (such as Tinkyada)
¼ cup cornstarch
4 cups 1% low-fat milk, divided
¾ teaspoon salt
½ teaspoon black pepper
½ teaspoon grated whole nutmeg
1 cup (4 ounces) shredded reduced-fat sharp cheddar cheese
1 cup (4 ounces) shredded part-skim mozzarella cheese
Cooking spray
½ cup (2 ounces) grated fresh Parmesan cheese
¼ cup panko-style breadcrumbs (such as Kinnikinnick)

1. Preheat oven to 375°.
2. Heat oil in a medium Dutch oven over medium heat. Add onion; cook 5 minutes or until tender, stirring often.
3. While onion cooks, cook pasta according to package directions, omitting salt and fat. Drain.
4. Combine cornstarch and ½ cup milk in a small bowl. Add remaining 3½ cups milk to onion; bring to a boil. Gradually stir in cornstarch mixture. Cook 2 minutes or until sauce thickens, stirring constantly. Remove from heat, and stir in salt, pepper, and nutmeg. Add cheddar and mozzarella cheeses, stirring with a whisk until cheeses melt. Stir in pasta. Pour pasta mixture evenly into 6 (2-cup) gratin dishes or ramekins coated with cooking spray.
5. Combine Parmesan cheese and breadcrumbs; sprinkle over pasta mixture. Bake at 375° for 30 minutes or until sauce is bubbly and top is brown. **Yield: 6 servings (serving size: about 1¼ cups).**

CALORIES 493; FAT 14.5g (sat 7.7g, mono 3.4g, poly 0.5g); PROTEIN 23.4g; CARB 67.1g; FIBER 2.1g; CHOL 40mg; IRON 3.8mg; SODIUM 308mg; CALC 767mg

Roasted Vegetable Pasta

This aromatic, colorful, and delicious pasta will please your senses of smell, sight, and taste.

- 3 cups (8 ounces) uncooked gluten-free multigrain penne (such as DeBoles)
- 1 (8-ounce) package baby portobello mushrooms, halved
- 2 cups grape or cherry tomatoes
- 1 red onion, sliced
- 1 tablespoon olive oil
- ½ teaspoon salt
- ¼ teaspoon freshly ground black pepper
- ¼ cup dry white wine
- 1 cup frozen petite green peas, thawed
- ¼ cup chopped fresh parsley
- ¼ cup (1½ ounces) thinly shaved fresh Parmesan cheese

1. Preheat oven to 475°.

2. Cook pasta according to package directions, omitting salt and fat. Drain and keep warm.

3. Combine mushrooms and next 5 ingredients in a bowl; toss well to coat. Arrange mushroom mixture in a single layer on a jelly-roll pan.

4. Bake at 475° for 15 minutes; turn vegetables over. Drizzle wine evenly over vegetables; bake an additional 7 minutes or until vegetables are tender and lightly browned. Combine pasta, vegetables, and peas in a large bowl. Top with parsley and cheese. **Yield: 4 servings (serving size: 1½ cups pasta and 1 tablespoon cheese).**

CALORIES 340; FAT 6.2g (sat 1.5g, mono 2.5g, poly 0.4g); PROTEIN 11.1g; CARB 59.4g; FIBER 4g; CHOL 5mg; IRON 4.7mg; SODIUM 478mg; CALC 174mg

Cooking Tip

Few cooking methods do as much as roasting to build big, intense flavors with such little effort. Baked in at least 400° heat, vegetables release moisture as they cook. As a result, their flavor becomes concentrated, and their natural sweetness comes out. Simply coat the vegetables with cooking spray or toss with oil or melted butter, and then toss with seasonings. Spread the vegetables in an even layer on a jelly-roll pan, baking pan, or roasting pan so they'll cook evenly. If the vegetables are not in a single layer, the ones on the bottom might steam rather than roast. Stir the vegetables occasionally as they roast.

Tomato-Basil Pasta with Asiago

You can substitute ½ teaspoon crushed dried rosemary for the fresh, if you'd like.

2 cups (6 ounces) uncooked gluten-free rice penne (such as DeBoles)
¾ cup canned no-salt-added navy beans, rinsed and drained
2 tablespoons extra-virgin olive oil
1 cup grape tomatoes, halved
¼ cup finely chopped green onions
½ teaspoon minced fresh rosemary
12 pitted kalamata olives, coarsely chopped
2 garlic cloves, minced
2 cups fresh baby spinach, coarsely chopped
¾ cup (3 ounces) grated Asiago cheese
¼ cup chopped fresh basil
½ teaspoon salt
½ teaspoon black pepper

1. Cook pasta according to package directions, omitting salt and fat; add beans during last 1 minute of cooking. Drain pasta and beans, reserving ¼ cup pasta water. Place pasta, beans, and reserved pasta water in a large shallow pasta bowl.

2. While pasta cooks, heat oil in a medium nonstick skillet over medium heat. Add tomatoes; cook 2 minutes, stirring often. Stir in green onions and next 3 ingredients; cook 2 minutes or just until tomatoes are thoroughly heated. Remove from heat.

3. Add spinach and next 4 ingredients to pasta mixture. Toss well. Top with tomato mixture. **Yield: 4 servings (serving size: 1⅓ cups).**

CALORIES 394; FAT 17.4g (sat 5.2g, mono 7.7g, poly 1g); PROTEIN 11.2g; CARB 47.7g; FIBER 4.5g; CHOL 19mg; IRON 4.4mg; SODIUM 718mg; CALC 243mg

Cooking Tip

You can easily strip rosemary leaves from their tough, inedible stems by holding the top of a stem in one hand, and then pulling in the opposite direction of the way the leaves grow.

Fresh Tomato, Sausage, and Pecorino Pasta

{Check for **Gluten**}

Ripe, late-summer tomatoes are juicy and delicious in this entrée, with no seeding or peeling necessary.

3 cups (8 ounces) uncooked gluten-free multigrain penne (such as DeBoles)

8 ounces sweet Italian sausage

2 teaspoons olive oil

1 cup vertically sliced onion

2 teaspoons minced garlic

1¼ pounds tomatoes, chopped

6 tablespoons grated fresh pecorino Romano cheese, divided

¼ teaspoon salt

⅛ teaspoon freshly ground black pepper

¼ cup torn fresh basil leaves

1. Cook pasta according to package directions, omitting salt and fat. Drain and keep warm.

2. Heat a large nonstick skillet over medium-high heat. Remove casings from sausage. Add oil to pan; swirl to coat. Add sausage and onion to pan; cook 4 minutes, stirring to crumble sausage. Add garlic; cook 2 minutes. Stir in tomatoes; cook 2 minutes. Remove from heat; stir in pasta, 2 tablespoons cheese, salt, and pepper. Sprinkle with remaining ¼ cup cheese and basil. **Yield: 4 servings (serving size: about 2 cups pasta, 1 tablespoon cheese, and 1 tablespoon basil).**

CALORIES 393; FAT 10.5g (sat 4.2g, mono 3.8g, poly 0.7g); PROTEIN 17.5g; CARB 55.8g; FIBER 2.3g; CHOL 24mg; IRON 4.7mg; SODIUM 665mg; CALC 211mg

Pasta with Roasted Red Pepper and Cream Sauce

Roasted red peppers and cream sauce deliver rich flavor in this quick and easy pasta recipe. Balsamic vinegar helps balance the natural sweetness of the red peppers.

1 pound uncooked gluten-free seashell pasta (such as Tinkyada)
2 teaspoons extra-virgin olive oil
½ cup finely chopped onion
1 (12-ounce) bottle roasted red bell peppers, drained and coarsely chopped
2 teaspoons balsamic vinegar
1 cup half-and-half
1 tablespoon tomato paste
⅛ teaspoon ground red pepper
1 cup (4 ounces) grated fresh Parmigiano-Reggiano cheese, divided
Thinly sliced fresh basil (optional)

1. Cook pasta according to package directions, omitting salt and fat. Drain and keep warm.

2. Heat oil in a large skillet over medium heat. Add onion, and cook 8 minutes or until tender, stirring frequently. Add bell peppers; cook 2 minutes or until thoroughly heated. Increase heat to medium-high. Stir in vinegar; cook 1 minute or until liquid evaporates. Remove from heat; cool 5 minutes.

3. Place bell pepper mixture in a blender; process until smooth. Return bell pepper mixture to pan; cook over low heat until warm. Combine half-and-half and tomato paste in a small bowl, stirring with a whisk. Stir tomato mixture into bell pepper mixture, stirring with a whisk until well combined. Stir in ground red pepper.

4. Combine pasta and bell pepper mixture in a large bowl. Add ½ cup cheese, tossing to coat. Spoon 1⅓ cups pasta into each of 6 bowls; top each serving with about 1½ tablespoons cheese. Garnish with basil, if desired. **Yield: 6 servings.**

CALORIES 442; FAT 12.3g (sat 6.4g, mono 2.8g, poly 0.4g); PROTEIN 14g; CARB 66.8g; FIBER 0.4g; CHOL 32mg; IRON 4.9mg; SODIUM 422mg; CALC 305mg

My family liked this dish very much and thought it was very satisfying and filling. We usually have spaghetti with a meat sauce, so it was a real treat to have delicious meatballs, which held together well and didn't fall apart. The recipe makes plenty for a family dinner or for a small family to enjoy another meal from the leftovers.

—Linda Kline

Spaghetti and Meatballs

{Check for **Gluten**}

Serve this pasta with the rest of the gluten-free baguette to round out your meal.

1 (1.5-ounce) slice gluten-free baguette
1 garlic clove
½ small onion, cut into 3 wedges
½ cup fresh parsley leaves
1 pound ground round
2 (4-ounce) links sweet turkey Italian sausage, casings removed
¼ cup (1 ounce) grated fresh Parmesan cheese
¼ cup fat-free, lower-sodium chicken broth
1 large egg
½ teaspoon freshly ground black pepper
¼ teaspoon crushed red pepper
Cooking spray
12 ounces uncooked gluten-free spaghetti
2 (25.5-ounce) jars gluten-free Italian herb pasta sauce
Chopped fresh parsley (optional)
Grated fresh Parmesan cheese (optional)

1. Preheat oven to 400°.

2. Place bread in a food processor; pulse 10 times or until coarse crumbs measure ½ cup. Transfer to a bowl; set aside.

3. Place garlic, onion, and parsley in processor; pulse 20 seconds or until chopped. Add breadcrumbs, ground round, and next 6 ingredients. Pulse 1 minute or until mixture is combined, stopping frequently to scrape down sides.

4. Line a broiler pan with foil. Shape meat mixture into 48 (1½-inch) balls. Place meatballs on broiler rack coated with cooking spray. Bake at 400° for 12 minutes or until meatballs are no longer pink in center.

5. While meatballs cook, cook pasta according to package directions, omitting salt and fat.

6. Bring pasta sauce to a simmer in a large saucepan. Add meatballs, and simmer 10 minutes or until sauce reaches desired consistency. Serve over spaghetti. Garnish with chopped parsley, and serve with additional Parmesan cheese, if desired.

Yield: 8 servings (serving size: ¾ cup pasta and 1 cup plus 2 tablespoons meatballs and sauce).

CALORIES 452; FAT 14.3g (sat 4.8g, mono 5.2g, poly 1.2g); PROTEIN 23.8g; CARB 53.9g; FIBER 3.2g; CHOL 96mg; IRON 6.7mg; SODIUM 850mg; CALC 111mg

Teriyaki Pork and Vegetables with Noodles

☑ Dairy **free**
{Check for **Gluten**}

The sweet-savory flavor of teriyaki sauce is a centuries-old mixture of soy sauce and mirin (sweet cooking wine). Over time, Japanese Americans added ginger, brown sugar, pineapple juice, and green onions, elements of the bottled teriyaki sauce Americans know today.

8 ounces uncooked gluten-free spaghetti
4 green onions
1 tablespoon dark sesame oil
1 cup thinly sliced red bell pepper
3 (4-ounce) boneless center-cut loin pork chops (about ½ inch thick), cut into ¼-inch strips
1 (3½-ounce) package shiitake mushrooms, sliced
⅓ cup low-sodium teriyaki sauce
4 teaspoons chili garlic sauce

1. Cook pasta according to package directions, omitting salt and fat. Drain, reserving ¼ cup pasta water; keep warm.

2. Remove green tops from green onions; thinly slice, and set aside. Mince white portions of green onions; set aside.

3. Heat oil in a large nonstick skillet over medium-high heat. Add minced green onions, bell pepper, pork, and mushrooms; sauté 3 minutes or until pork is browned. Combine reserved ¼ cup pasta water, teriyaki sauce, and chili garlic sauce in a small bowl, stirring with a whisk. Add pasta and teriyaki sauce mixture to pan; toss well to coat. Stir in sliced green onion tops. **Yield: 4 servings (serving size: about 1¾ cups).**

CALORIES 377; FAT 8.4g (sat 1.8g, mono 2.9g, poly 2g); PROTEIN 21.1g; CARB 52.2g; FIBER 1.1g; CHOL 50mg; IRON 4.5mg; SODIUM 469mg; CALC 66mg

Pasta Carbonara Florentine

Whisked eggs and Parmesan cheese are stirred into a skillet of just-cooked pasta to coat the noodles with a rich, creamy sauce. The spinach isn't traditional but adds color and a subtle earthy flavor twist.

6 center-cut bacon slices, chopped
1 cup finely chopped onion
2 tablespoons dry white wine
1 (6-ounce) package bagged prewashed baby spinach
8 ounces uncooked gluten-free spaghetti
½ cup (2 ounces) grated fresh Parmesan cheese
½ teaspoon salt
½ teaspoon freshly ground black pepper
1 large egg
1 large egg white
3 tablespoons chopped fresh parsley

1. Heat a large nonstick skillet over medium heat. Add bacon to pan; cook 5 minutes or until crisp, stirring frequently. Remove bacon from pan, reserving 2 teaspoons drippings in pan; set bacon aside.

2. Add onion to drippings in pan; cook 3 minutes or until tender, stirring frequently. Add wine; cook 1 minute or until liquid is reduced by half. Add spinach; cook 1 minute or until spinach wilts, stirring constantly. Remove from heat; keep warm.

3. Cook pasta according to package directions, omitting salt and fat. Drain well, reserving 1 tablespoon pasta water. Immediately add pasta and reserved pasta water to spinach mixture in pan. Add reserved bacon; stir well to combine. Place pan over low heat.

4. Combine cheese and next 4 ingredients, stirring with a whisk. Add to pasta mixture, tossing well to coat. Cook 1 minute. Remove from heat. Sprinkle with parsley. Serve immediately. **Yield: 4 servings (serving size: 1 cup).**

CALORIES 373; FAT 9.8g (sat 4.3g, mono 2.5g, poly 0.5g); PROTEIN 16.1g; CARB 55.1g; FIBER 2.8g; CHOL 72mg; IRON 5.6mg; SODIUM 773mg; CALC 257mg

Artichoke and Feta Pasta Salad

Letting the pasta salad stand for 10 minutes before serving will give the flavors time to blend.

2⅓ cups (6 ounces) uncooked gluten-free brown rice rotini (corkscrew pasta)
¼ cup red wine vinegar
2 tablespoons extra-virgin olive oil
½ teaspoon salt
⅛ teaspoon crushed red pepper
3 garlic cloves, minced
1 cup matchstick-cut red bell pepper
½ cup finely chopped red onion
¼ cup chopped fresh basil
1 (14-ounce) can quartered artichoke hearts, drained and coarsely chopped
1 (15-ounce) can no-salt-added chickpeas (garbanzo beans), rinsed and drained
3 ounces feta cheese, crumbled

1. Cook pasta according to package directions, omitting salt and fat. Drain and rinse with cold running water until cool. Drain.
2. Combine vinegar and next 4 ingredients in a large bowl. Add pasta, bell pepper, and next 4 ingredients. Toss well. Add cheese; toss gently. Let stand 10 minutes. **Yield: 6 servings (serving size: 1⅓ cups).**

CALORIES 266; FAT 8.3g (sat 2.8g, mono 4.3g, poly 0.6g); PROTEIN 7.4g; CARB 39.6g; FIBER 4.4g; CHOL 13mg; IRON 1mg; SODIUM 674mg; CALC 103mg

Spicy Shrimp Noodle Bowl

☑ Dairy **free**

{Check for **Gluten**}

Chili garlic sauce adds some great kick to this Asian-inspired noodle dish, perfect for a quick weeknight dinner. If you don't have chili garlic sauce, substitute ½ teaspoon crushed red pepper.

1 pound tail-on peeled and deveined medium shrimp
1½ cups water
1 cup fat-free, lower-sodium chicken broth
1 (8-ounce) bottle clam juice
2 (¼-inch-thick) slices peeled fresh ginger
1 teaspoon olive oil
¾ cup thinly sliced red bell pepper
¼ cup thinly sliced yellow onion
1 garlic clove, minced
½ cup sugar snap peas
2 teaspoons chili garlic sauce
¼ teaspoon salt
3 ounces uncooked rice sticks (rice-flour noodles)
2 tablespoons fresh cilantro leaves
Lime wedges

1. Remove shrimp tails; set shrimp aside. Combine shrimp tails, 1½ cups water, and next 3 ingredients in a saucepan; bring to a boil. Reduce heat, and simmer, uncovered, 10 minutes. Strain broth mixture through a sieve into a bowl; discard solids.

2. Heat olive oil in a medium saucepan over medium-high heat. Add bell pepper, yellow onion, and garlic; sauté 3 minutes. Add reserved broth; bring to a simmer. Add shrimp, peas, and next 3 ingredients; cook 5 minutes or until noodles are done. Ladle 1¼ cups soup into each of 4 bowls; top each serving with 1½ teaspoons cilantro. Serve with lime wedges. **Yield: 4 servings.**

CALORIES 236; FAT 3.6g (sat 0.7g, mono 1.3g, poly 1g); PROTEIN 26.5g; CARB 25.4g; FIBER 1.9g; CHOL 174mg; IRON 3.7mg; SODIUM 506mg; CALC 84mg

Vietnamese Beef-Noodle Soup with Asian Greens

☑ Dairy **free**
{Check for **Gluten**}

Introduce your taste buds to Vietnamese cuisine with this quick and easy soup. The rich broth, aromatic herbs, and tender steak will leave you wanting more.

1 (8-ounce) boneless sirloin steak
4 ounces uncooked wide rice sticks (rice-flour noodles)
1½ cups thinly sliced yellow onion
3 whole cloves
2 cardamom pods
2 garlic cloves, halved
1 (3-inch) piece peeled fresh ginger, thinly sliced
1 star anise
3 cups fat-free, lower-sodium beef broth
3 cups water
1 tablespoon lower-sodium soy sauce
1 teaspoon brown sugar
2 teaspoons fish sauce (such as Thai Kitchen)
4 cups baby bok choy leaves
1 cup snow peas, trimmed
1 small Thai chile, thinly sliced into rings
1 cup fresh bean sprouts
¼ cup fresh basil leaves
¼ cup fresh mint leaves
4 lime wedges

1. Freeze beef 10 minutes; cut across grain into ⅛-inch-thick slices.

2. Cook noodles according to package directions. Drain and rinse with cold water; drain.

3. Place onion and next 5 ingredients in a large saucepan; cook over medium-high heat 5 minutes, stirring frequently. Add broth and 3 cups water; bring to a boil. Strain broth mixture through a fine sieve over a bowl; discard solids. Return broth to pan. Add soy sauce, sugar, and fish sauce; bring to a boil. Add bok choy and snow peas; simmer 4 minutes or until peas are crisp-tender and bok choy wilts.

4. Arrange ½ cup noodles in each of 4 large bowls. Divide raw beef and chile slices evenly among bowls. Ladle about 1⅔ cups hot soup over each serving (broth will cook beef). Top each serving with ¼ cup bean sprouts, 1 tablespoon basil, and 1 tablespoon mint. Serve with lime wedges. **Yield: 4 servings.**

CALORIES 262; FAT 4.3g (sat 1.6g, mono 1.5g, poly 0.4g); PROTEIN 17.5g; CARB 37.7g; FIBER 3.8g; CHOL 28mg; IRON 3.9mg; SODIUM 777mg; CALC 131mg

Cooking Tip

Freezing the beef for just 10 minutes makes it easier to cut into thin ⅛-inch slices, so it's worth taking the time to complete that step.

Spicy Asian Noodles with Chicken

☑ Dairy **free**
{Check for **Gluten**}

Bring the flavor of your favorite takeout to the dinner table in no time. Add a snow pea sauté to complete the meal.

1 tablespoon dark sesame oil, divided
1 tablespoon grated peeled fresh ginger
2 garlic cloves, minced
2 cups chopped cooked skinless, boneless chicken breasts
½ cup chopped green onions
¼ cup chopped fresh cilantro
3 tablespoons lower-sodium soy sauce
2 tablespoons rice vinegar
2 tablespoons hoisin sauce
2 teaspoons chile paste with garlic (such as sambal oelek)
1 (6.75-ounce) package thin rice sticks (rice-flour noodles)
2 tablespoons chopped dry-roasted peanuts

1. Heat 2 teaspoons oil in a small skillet over medium-high heat. Add ginger and garlic to pan; cook 45 seconds, stirring constantly. Place in a large bowl. Stir in remaining 1 teaspoon oil, chicken, and next 6 ingredients.

2. Cook noodles according to package directions. Drain and rinse under cold water; drain. Cut noodles into smaller pieces. Add noodles to bowl; toss well to coat. Sprinkle with peanuts.

Yield: 4 servings (serving size: 1¾ cups).

CALORIES 381; FAT 8.1g (sat 1.5g, mono 3.2g, poly 2.7g); PROTEIN 27.5g; CARB 47.1g; FIBER 2.3g; CHOL 60mg; IRON 3.1mg; SODIUM 614mg; CALC 55mg

Cooking Tip

If you purchase deli-roasted chicken from the grocery store, be sure to ask about the ingredients used when preparing it. Some stores use flour in the seasoning that coats it.

Sandwiches
& Soups

Cornmeal-Crusted Tilapia Sandwiches with Lime Butter

Serve this hearty sandwich with grapes and coleslaw for a weeknight supper.

3 tablespoons yellow cornmeal (such as Bob's Red Mill)
1 tablespoon chili powder
1 teaspoon ground cumin
½ teaspoon ground coriander
¼ teaspoon salt
⅛ teaspoon ground red pepper
4 (6-ounce) tilapia fillets
Cooking spray
4 teaspoons butter, softened
1 teaspoon grated lime rind
½ teaspoon fresh lime juice
1 (10-ounce) gluten-free baguette, halved lengthwise, toasted, and cut into 4 pieces
1 cup shredded red leaf lettuce
8 (¼-inch-thick) slices tomato

1. Preheat broiler.
2. Combine first 6 ingredients in a shallow dish. Coat both sides of fish with cooking spray. Dredge fish in cornmeal mixture.
3. Place fish on a broiler pan coated with cooking spray. Broil 10 minutes or until desired degree of doneness.
4. Combine butter, rind, and juice in a small bowl; stir well.
5. Spread 1 teaspoon butter mixture over cut side of each of 4 bread tops. Place ¼ cup lettuce, 2 tomato slices, and 1 fillet on each of 4 roll bottoms. Place top halves of rolls on sandwiches.

Yield: 4 servings (serving size: 1 sandwich).

CALORIES 447; FAT 14.4g (sat 3.6g, mono 4.6g, poly 3.7g); PROTEIN 39.4g; CARB 41.3g; FIBER 0.8g; CHOL 159mg; IRON 2.9mg; SODIUM 680mg; CALC 127mg

Cooking Tip

Coating the broiler pan with cooking spray is an important step to ensure the coating stays on the fish, not stuck to the pan. Be sure not to overcrowd the pan either. Overcrowding can hinder evaporation as the food cooks, creating steam and ultimately a soggy crust.

Tuna-Pecan Salad Sandwiches

1 (12-ounce) can albacore tuna in water, drained
⅓ cup chopped celery
⅓ cup diced Gala apple (about 1 small)
⅓ cup fat-free mayonnaise
¼ cup chopped pecans, toasted
¼ teaspoon salt
¼ teaspoon black pepper
4 curly leaf lettuce leaves
4 gluten-free English muffins, split and toasted

1. Combine first 7 ingredients in a small bowl. Place a lettuce leaf on half of each English muffin. Top evenly with tuna salad. Top with remaining English muffin halves. **Yield: 4 servings (serving size: 1 sandwich).**

CALORIES 302; FAT 9.5 (sat 1g, mono 3.7g, poly 3.6g); PROTEIN 17.5g; CARB 46.5g; FIBER 3.5g; CHOL 18mg; IRON 4.1mg; SODIUM 752mg; CALC 19mg

Cooking Tip

To enhance browning when toasting gluten-free English muffins, coat the muffins with cooking spray, and then toast them in a toaster oven or underneath a broiler to get the best browning results.

Steak and Fennel Sandwiches

½ teaspoon salt
½ teaspoon ground fennel seeds
¼ teaspoon ground cumin
¼ teaspoon freshly ground black pepper
4 teaspoons olive oil, divided
3 cups thinly sliced fennel bulb (about 1 bulb)
4 (4-ounce) beef tenderloin steaks, trimmed (1 inch thick)
8 teaspoons light mayonnaise
8 (1-ounce) slices gluten-free bread, lightly toasted
1 cup arugula

1. Combine salt, ground fennel seeds, ground cumin, and black pepper in a small bowl.

2. Heat 2 teaspoons oil in a large nonstick skillet over medium-high heat. Add ½ teaspoon spice mixture and fennel; sauté 15 minutes or until fennel is tender and lightly browned. Transfer to a bowl; wipe pan clean with paper towels.

3. Heat remaining 2 teaspoons oil in pan; sprinkle steaks evenly with remaining spice mixture. Add steaks to pan; cook 4 minutes on each side or until desired degree of doneness. Remove from pan; let stand 10 minutes. Thinly slice steaks.

4. To prepare sandwiches, spread 2 teaspoons mayonnaise onto each of 4 bread slices. Top each with one-fourth of beef, one-fourth of fennel, and ¼ cup arugula. Top with remaining 4 bread slices. **Yield: 4 servings (serving size: 1 sandwich).**

CALORIES 408; FAT 18.4g (sat 5.9g, mono 6.3g, poly 0.8g); PROTEIN 27.1g; CARB 29.5g; FIBER 6.1g; CHOL 79mg; IRON 2.5mg; SODIUM 726mg; CALC 69mg

Cooking Tip

When buying fennel, look for small, heavy, white bulbs that are firm and free of cracks, browning, or moist areas. The stalks should be crisp, with feathery, bright-green fronds. Wrapped in plastic, fennel keeps for just a few days in the refrigerator; the flavor fades as it dries out.

Banh Mi–Style Roast Beef Sandwiches

{Check for **Gluten**}

⅛ teaspoon kosher salt

⅛ teaspoon freshly ground black pepper

¾ pound flank steak, trimmed

2 tablespoons rice vinegar

1 tablespoon fish sauce (such as Thai Kitchen)

1 tablespoon lower-sodium soy sauce

1½ teaspoons sugar

1 jalapeño pepper, thinly sliced

1 cup matchstick-cut carrots

½ cup thinly sliced radishes

1 (7.5-ounce) gluten-free baguette, halved lengthwise and toasted

½ cup fresh cilantro leaves

1. Heat a large cast-iron skillet over medium-high heat. Sprinkle salt and pepper evenly over steak. Add steak to pan; cook 5 minutes on each side or until desired degree of doneness. Remove steak from pan; let stand 5 minutes. Cut steak diagonally across grain into thin slices.

2. While steak cooks, combine vinegar and next 4 ingredients in a medium bowl. Combine carrots and radishes in a medium bowl; add 1 tablespoon vinegar mixture, tossing to coat. Let vegetable mixture stand 5 minutes. Add steak to remaining 5 tablespoons vinegar mixture; toss well to coat.

3. Arrange steak on bottom half of bread; top with vegetable mixture and cilantro. Top with top half of bread; cut into 4 equal pieces. **Yield: 4 servings (serving size: 1 sandwich).**

CALORIES 355; FAT 12.8g (sat 2.9g, mono 4.8g, poly 2.5g); PROTEIN 27.9g; CARB 31.4g; FIBER 0.7g; CHOL 98mg; IRON 2.8mg; SODIUM 896mg; CALC 102mg

Pork Wraps with Fresh Tomatillo Salsa

2 large tomatillos
½ cup chopped cucumber
¼ cup chopped fresh cilantro
2 tablespoons fresh lime juice
½ teaspoon salt, divided
1 garlic clove, peeled
Cooking spray
1 pound boneless pork cutlets, cut into thin strips
1 teaspoon ground cumin
2 medium poblano chiles, stemmed, seeded, and cut into thin strips
1 medium onion, vertically sliced
4 (8-inch) gluten-free tortillas
½ cup light sour cream

1. Discard husks and stems from tomatillos. Place tomatillos, cucumber, cilantro, lime juice, ¼ teaspoon salt, and garlic in a blender. Process until finely chopped, and set aside.

2. Heat a large nonstick skillet over medium-high heat. Coat pan with cooking spray. Sprinkle pork with cumin. Add pork to pan; cook 3 minutes or until no longer pink in center, stirring occasionally. Remove from pan; keep warm.

3. Recoat pan with cooking spray; add chiles and onion. Coat vegetables with cooking spray; cook 4 minutes or until onion begins to brown, stirring frequently.

4. While vegetables cook, warm tortillas.

5. Return pork to pan; add remaining ¼ teaspoon salt, and cook 30 seconds or until pork mixture is thoroughly heated, stirring constantly.

6. Divide pork mixture evenly among tortillas. Top each with about ⅓ cup salsa; roll up. Serve with sour cream. **Yield: 4 servings (serving size: 1 wrap and 2 tablespoons sour cream).**

CALORIES 350; FAT 10.1g (sat 3.2g, mono 2.9g, poly 2.4g); PROTEIN 28.6g; CARB 35.6g; FIBER 5.6g; CHOL 85mg; IRON 3.1mg; SODIUM 468mg; CALC 57mg

Cooking Tip

Since gluten-free tortillas are stored in the refrigerator, they'll need to be warmed to prevent breaking. Steam them by placing each tortilla on a splatter guard set over a pan of simmering water. Cover with a lid, and heat about 5 to 10 seconds or until they're soft and pliable. They're best when filled and eaten immediately after steaming.

Ham, Cheese, and Apple Panini

{Check for **Gluten**}

If you don't have a panini press, you can make these easy sandwiches in a nonstick skillet, much like you make grilled cheese sandwiches.

1 tablespoon apple jelly
¼ cup Dijon mustard
8 (1-ounce) slices gluten-free bread
8 slices lower-sodium deli ham (6 ounces)
4 (0.8-ounce) cheddar cheese or cheddar-flavored nondairy slices
1 Granny Smith apple, cored and cut into 24 thin slices
Butter-flavored cooking spray

1. Preheat panini press.

2. Microwave jelly at HIGH 10 seconds or until it melts. Combine jelly and mustard; spread mixture evenly over 1 side of 4 bread slices. Layer 2 ham slices, 1 cheese slice, and 6 apple slices over mustard mixture on each bread slice; top evenly with remaining bread slices.

3. Coat sandwiches with cooking spray. Add sandwiches, 2 at a time, to panini press; grill 2 minutes or until toasted. **Yield: 4 servings (serving size: 1 sandwich).**

CALORIES 261; FAT 6g (sat 2g, mono 0.3, poly 0.6g); PROTEIN 9.7g; CARB 39g; FIBER 4.4g; CHOL 19mg; IRON 0.3mg; SODIUM 849mg; CALC 202mg

Bacon, Spinach, and Red Onion Sandwiches with Raspberry-Chipotle Mustard

{Check for **Gluten**}

3 tablespoons seedless raspberry fruit spread
1½ tablespoons country-style Dijon mustard
1 tablespoon canola oil
1 tablespoon chopped chipotle chile, canned in adobo sauce
8 (1-ounce) slices gluten-free bread, lightly toasted
8 center-cut bacon slices, cooked
4 thin slices red onion
2 cups baby spinach

1. Combine first 4 ingredients in a small bowl, stirring well. Spread mustard mixture evenly on 4 toast slices.

2. Top evenly with bacon, onion, spinach, and remaining bread slices, pressing down slightly. **Yield: 4 servings (serving size: 1 sandwich).**

CALORIES 259; FAT 9.2g (sat 3.3g, mono 2.2g, poly 1g); PROTEIN 5.4g; CARB 35.7g; FIBER 5.1g; CHOL 10mg; IRON 0.5mg; SODIUM 629mg; CALC 12mg

This sandwich is very easy to make and has a great combo of sweet, savory, salty, and spicy. This relish is also delicious spread on a panini sandwich with grilled, sliced chicken and cheese.

—*Martine Giddings*

Chicken-Arugula Salad Open-Faced Sandwiches

2 tablespoons extra-virgin olive oil

1 tablespoon red wine vinegar

1 teaspoon fresh or dried rosemary, crushed

½ teaspoon dried oregano

¼ teaspoon salt

¼ teaspoon crushed red pepper

2 garlic cloves, minced

2 cups diced cooked chicken breast

¼ cup finely chopped red onion

6 tablespoons (1½ ounces) crumbled reduced-fat feta cheese

4 (1-ounce) slices gluten-free bread, lightly toasted

2 cups packed arugula

1 (6-ounce) tomato, cut into 4 slices

1. Combine first 7 ingredients in a medium bowl, stirring with a whisk. Add chicken, onion, and cheese, tossing gently.

2. Place 1 toast slice on each of 4 plates. Top each with ½ cup arugula, 1 tomato slice, and about ½ cup chicken mixture.

Yield: 4 servings (serving size: 1 sandwich).

CALORIES 289; FAT 12.7g (sat 3.7g, mono 6.3g, poly 1.3g); PROTEIN 25.3g; CARB 16.1g; FIBER 3.2g; CHOL 63mg; IRON 1.2mg; SODIUM 480mg; CALC 73mg

Cooking Tip

Arugula has a peppery flavor that's more intense than that of most lettuces. It's highly perishable and will only last for a few days after purchase. Store it in the refrigerator inside a perforated plastic bag. Rinse thoroughly, and pat dry before using.

Chicken and Mint Coleslaw Wraps

☑ Dairy **free**

4 (6-ounce) skinless, boneless chicken breast halves
⅛ teaspoon salt
Cooking spray
⅓ cup fresh lemon juice (about 2 lemons)
1 tablespoon bottled ground fresh ginger
2 teaspoons sugar
¼ teaspoon crushed red pepper
3 cups angel hair coleslaw
½ cup chopped fresh mint
1 poblano chile, halved lengthwise, seeded, and thinly sliced
6 (8-inch) gluten-free tortillas

1. Place each chicken breast half between 2 sheets of heavy-duty plastic wrap; pound to ¼-inch thickness using a meat mallet or small heavy skillet. Sprinkle chicken with salt. Heat a large nonstick skillet coated with cooking spray over medium-high heat. Add chicken; sauté 4½ minutes on each side or until done. Remove chicken to a cutting board, and cut into thin strips.

2. Combine juice and next 3 ingredients in a large bowl. Add chicken strips, coleslaw, mint, and chile, tossing well to coat. Warm tortillas according to package directions. Divide chicken mixture evenly among tortillas; roll up. Cut each rolled tortilla in half crosswise. **Yield: 6 servings (serving size: 2 tortilla halves).**

CALORIES 288; FAT 4.4g (sat 0.5g, mono 1.1g, poly 1.8g); PROTEIN 29.3g; CARB 31g; FIBER 4g; CHOL 66mg; IRON 2.6mg; SODIUM 293mg; CALC 32mg

Cooking Tip

Before juicing, roll a room-temperature lemon under your palm to break down the cells inside the fruit that hold the liquid. If the lemon is particularly hard, microwave it for 20 seconds. You should get 2 to 3 tablespoons of lemon juice per fruit.

Spicy Chicken Sandwiches with Cilantro-Lime Mayo

Chicken cutlets are encrusted with tortilla chip crumbs, which yield a satisfying crunch. You can also use spicy chips for more heat.

¼ cup reduced-fat mayonnaise
2 tablespoons chopped fresh cilantro
1 teaspoon fresh lime juice
1 garlic clove, minced
2 egg whites, lightly beaten
3 tablespoons hot pepper sauce (such as Tabasco)
1 teaspoon dried oregano
½ teaspoon salt
2 (6-ounce) skinless, boneless chicken breast halves
4½ ounces gluten-free tortilla chips (about 6 cups)
2 tablespoons olive oil
4 (1.5-ounce) gluten-free sandwich rolls
12 (⅛-inch-thick) slices red onion
4 lettuce leaves

1. Combine first 4 ingredients; refrigerate until ready to prepare sandwiches.

2. Combine egg whites and next 3 ingredients in a large zip-top plastic bag. Cut chicken breast halves in half horizontally to form 4 cutlets. Add chicken to bag; seal. Marinate in refrigerator for at least 2 hours or up to 8 hours, turning bag occasionally.

3. Place tortilla chips in a food processor; process 1 minute or until ground. Place ground chips in a shallow dish.

4. Working with one cutlet at a time, remove chicken from bag, allowing excess marinade to drip off. Coat chicken completely in chips. Set aside. Repeat procedure with remaining chicken and chips.

5. Heat a large nonstick skillet over medium heat. Add oil to pan, swirling to coat. Add chicken to pan; cook 3 minutes on each side or until browned and done. Spread mayonnaise mixture evenly over cut sides of rolls. Layer bottom half of each roll with 3 onion slices, 1 lettuce leaf, and 1 chicken cutlet; top with top halves of rolls. **Yield: 4 servings (serving size: 1 sandwich).**

CALORIES 483; FAT 20.3g (sat 3.5g, mono 6.3g, poly 3.8g); PROTEIN 25.7g; CARB 50.5g; FIBER 6.7g; CHOL 49mg; IRON 1.4mg; SODIUM 889mg; CALC 49mg

Portobello and Black Bean Quesadillas

Sautéed portobellos are delicious in ragouts; as a topping for polenta or pizza; or as a filling for fajitas, tacos, or quesadillas. The portobello mushroom stands up to the robust flavors in these quesadillas, all the while preserving its own sturdy texture.

4 (8-inch) gluten-free tortillas
Butter-flavored cooking spray
2 (4½-inch) portobello caps, chopped
2 tablespoons light balsamic vinaigrette
1 cup canned no-salt-added black beans, rinsed and drained
1 (2-ounce) jar diced pimiento, drained
1 cup (4 ounces) shredded reduced-fat 4-cheese Mexican blend cheese
¼ cup thinly sliced green onions
Fresh salsa (optional)
Reduced-fat sour cream (optional)

1. Stack tortillas; microwave at HIGH 1 minute. Leave in microwave to keep warm while preparing filling.

2. Heat a large nonstick skillet over medium-high heat. Coat pan with cooking spray. Add mushrooms; sauté 2 minutes or until tender. Add vinaigrette, beans, and pimiento; cook 1 to 2 minutes or until liquid evaporates, stirring constantly. Mash bean mixture slightly with a potato masher.

3. Spoon about ⅓ cup bean mixture onto each tortilla. Sprinkle evenly with cheese and onions. Fold tortillas in half.

4. Wipe skillet with paper towels; heat over medium heat. Coat pan with cooking spray. Place 2 quesadillas in pan; cook 2 to 3 minutes on each side or until golden and cheese melts. Repeat procedure with remaining 2 quesadillas. Cut each quesadilla into 3 wedges. Serve immediately with salsa and sour cream, if desired. **Yield: 4 servings (serving size: 1 quesadilla).**

CALORIES 289; FAT 9.3g (sat 3.4g, mono 2.2g, poly 1.5g); PROTEIN 13.7g; CARB 37.7g; FIBER 6.1g; CHOL 18mg; IRON 2mg; SODIUM 512mg; CALC 364mg

Chicken-Olive Quesadillas

{Check for **Gluten**}

½ cup chopped cooked chicken
  breast
3 tablespoons sliced ripe olives
¼ teaspoon chili powder
¼ teaspoon ground cumin
¾ cup (3 ounces) shredded part-
  skim mozzarella cheese
1 (4.5-ounce) can chopped green
  chiles, drained
Butter-flavored cooking spray
4 (6-inch) corn tortillas
Fresh salsa (optional)
**Reduced-fat sour cream
  (optional)**

1. Combine first 6 ingredients in a medium bowl.

2. Heat a large nonstick skillet over medium-high heat. Coat pan with cooking spray. Add 1 tortilla to pan. Spread about ½ cup chicken mixture on left half of tortilla; fold right side of tortilla over filling, pressing gently with a spatula. Place an additional tortilla in pan, overlapping first quesadilla. Spread about ½ cup chicken mixture on right half of tortilla; fold left side of tortilla over filling, pressing with spatula. (Folded sides of tortillas should meet in center of pan.) Cook 1 minute.

3. Coat quesadillas with cooking spray; turn quesadillas over, keeping folded sides together in center of pan. Cook 1 to 2 minutes or until golden and cheese melts. Remove from pan; cover and keep warm. Repeat procedure with cooking spray and remaining tortillas and filling. Serve immediately with salsa and sour cream, if desired. **Yield: 4 servings (serving size: 1 quesadilla).**

CALORIES 178; FAT 6.3g (sat 1.4g, mono 2.6g, poly 1.8g); PROTEIN 11.8g; CARB 16.3g; FIBER 1.3g; CHOL 15mg; IRON 0.4mg; SODIUM 312mg; CALC 9mg

Chipotle Salmon Burgers

If you have a mini food processor, use it to prepare the mayonnaise mixture. You can use gluten-free English muffins if you don't have hamburger buns on hand.

1 tablespoon chopped fresh cilantro
3 tablespoons light mayonnaise
2 tablespoons finely chopped mango
1 tablespoon finely chopped pineapple
⅛ teaspoon finely grated lime rind
⅓ cup chopped green onions
¼ cup chopped fresh cilantro
1 tablespoon finely chopped chipotle chile, canned in adobo sauce
2 teaspoons fresh lime juice
¼ teaspoon salt
1 (1¼-pound) salmon fillet, skinned and cut into 1-inch pieces
Cooking spray
4 (2.8-ounce) gluten-free hamburger buns
4 butter lettuce leaves

1. Place first 5 ingredients in a food processor or blender; process until slightly chunky. Transfer to a bowl; cover and chill.

2. Place onions, ¼ cup cilantro, chile, and juice in a food processor; process until finely chopped. Add salt and fish; pulse 4 times or until fish is coarsely ground and mixture is well blended.

3. Divide fish mixture into 4 equal portions, shaping each into a 1-inch-thick patty. Cover and chill 30 minutes.

4. Heat a grill pan over medium-high heat. Coat pan with cooking spray. Add patties to pan; cook 6 minutes on each side or until desired degree of doneness.

5. Wipe pan with paper towels; recoat with cooking spray. Place 2 buns, cut sides down, in pan; cook 2 minutes or until lightly toasted. Repeat procedure with cooking spray and remaining buns.

6. Top bottom half of each bun with 1 lettuce leaf and 1 patty. Spread about 1 tablespoon mayonnaise mixture over each patty; place top half of 1 bun on each serving. **Yield: 4 servings (serving size: 1 burger).**

CALORIES 509; FAT 21.1g (sat 2.7g, mono 7.8g, poly 8.4g); PROTEIN 37.3g; CARB 39.7g; FIBER 4.9g; CHOL 99mg; IRON 3.4mg; SODIUM 682mg; CALC 50mg

Cooking Tip

Shape the patties up to 8 hours in advance, and cook just before serving. Use a grill pan or nonstick skillet to cook them since they may not hold up on a standard grill.

Cast-Iron Burgers

{Check for **Gluten**}

Patties:
- 1 pound ground sirloin
- ¼ teaspoon kosher salt

Horseradish Spread:
- 1 tablespoon canola mayonnaise
- 1 tablespoon Dijon mustard
- 1 tablespoon prepared horseradish
- 2 teaspoons ketchup

Relish:
- 2 applewood-smoked bacon slices, chopped
- 3 cups vertically sliced yellow onion
- 1 tablespoon finely chopped fresh chives
- 1 teaspoon Worcestershire sauce
- ¼ teaspoon freshly ground black pepper

Remaining Ingredients:
- Cooking spray
- 4 (2.8-ounce) gluten-free hamburger buns, toasted
- 4 green leaf lettuce leaves
- 4 (¼-inch-thick) slices tomato

1. To prepare patties, divide beef into 4 portions, lightly shaping each into a ½-inch-thick patty. Sprinkle evenly with salt. Cover and refrigerate 30 minutes.

2. To prepare horseradish spread, combine mayonnaise and next 3 ingredients in a small bowl. Set aside.

3. To prepare relish, cook bacon in a large nonstick skillet over medium-low heat until crisp. Remove bacon from pan. Add onion to drippings in pan; cook 15 minutes or until golden brown. Combine bacon, onion mixture, chives, Worcestershire sauce, and pepper in a small bowl.

4. Heat a large cast-iron skillet over medium-high heat. Coat pan with cooking spray. Add patties; cook 2 minutes on each side or until desired degree of doneness. Spread 1½ teaspoons horseradish spread on cut side of each bun half. Top bottom half of each bun with 1 lettuce leaf, 1 tomato slice, 1 patty, ¼ cup relish, and top half of bun. **Yield: 4 burgers (serving size: 1 burger).**

CALORIES 549; FAT 23.8g (sat 6.3g, mono 10g, poly 4.2g); PROTEIN 31.4g; CARB 51.1g; FIBER 6.8g; CHOL 85mg; IRON 5mg; SODIUM 816mg; CALC 77mg

The burgers were really good.
I love the addition of the onions cooked in the bacon drippings. We made it an open-faced burger and still enjoyed it with a few less calories!

—*Barbara Wallace*

Turkey Burgers with Cranberry-Peach Chutney

Enjoy the flavors of Thanksgiving all year long in this dressed-up turkey burger. Try grilling the burgers for an added boost of flavor. Serve with vegetable chips and red grapes.

⅓ cup prepared cranberry chutney
⅓ cup finely chopped peeled peaches
1 tablespoon finely chopped green onions
1 pound ground turkey breast
1 large egg white
¼ teaspoon salt
¼ teaspoon freshly ground black pepper
Cooking spray
4 lettuce leaves
4 (2.8-ounce) gluten-free hamburger buns, toasted

1. Combine first 3 ingredients in a small bowl, stirring well to blend. Set aside.

2. Combine turkey and next 3 ingredients. Divide turkey mixture into 4 equal portions, shaping each into a ½-inch-thick patty.

3. Heat a large nonstick skillet over medium heat. Coat pan with cooking spray. Add patties; cook 3 to 4 minutes on each side or until a thermometer registers 165°.

4. Place 1 lettuce leaf on bottom half of each bun; top each with 1 patty and 2 tablespoons cranberry mixture. Top each with 1 bun top. **Yield: 4 servings (serving size: 1 burger).**

CALORIES 420; FAT 8.8g (sat 1g, mono 3g, poly 3.2g); PROTEIN 32.7g; CARB 50g; FIBER 4.6g; CHOL 51mg; IRON 3.3mg; SODIUM 577mg; CALC 32mg

Cooking Tip

For this recipe, select ground turkey breast over ground turkey, which contains both the dark and white meat. The breast meat is much lower in calories and fat.

Chunky Tomato-Fruit Gazpacho

The mangoes, melons, and nectarines, along with the cucumber, give this gazpacho a sweet spin.

2 cups finely chopped tomato (about ¾ pound)
2 cups finely diced honeydew melon (about ¾ pound)
2 cups finely diced cantaloupe (about ¾ pound)
1 cup finely diced mango (about 1 medium)
1 cup finely diced seeded peeled cucumber (about 1 medium)
1 cup finely diced nectarines (about 3 medium)
1 cup fresh orange juice (about 4 oranges)
½ cup finely chopped Vidalia or other sweet onion
¼ cup chopped fresh basil
3 tablespoons chopped fresh mint
3 tablespoons fresh lemon juice
1 teaspoon sugar
½ teaspoon salt
1 jalapeño pepper, seeded and finely chopped
Crumbled feta cheese (optional)

1. Combine first 14 ingredients in a large bowl. Cover and chill at least 2 hours. Sprinkle cheese on top just before serving, if desired. **Yield: 7 servings (serving size: 1 cup).**

CALORIES 95; FAT 0.5g (sat 0.1g, mono 0.1g, poly 0.2g); PROTEIN 2.1g; CARB 23g; FIBER 2.8g; CHOL 0mg; IRON 0.9mg; SODIUM 189mg; CALC 33mg

Cooking Tip

Chile peppers like jalapeños can add depth to a recipe, but they also can add some heat. You can control the heat by removing as many or as few of the seeds as you'd like. Since capsaicin, the compound that gives peppers their kick, can stick to your hands, you should wear gloves when handling them.

Roasted Butternut Squash and Shallot Soup

☑ Dairy **free**
{Check for **Gluten**}

Spicy fresh ginger complements the sweet roasted winter squash and shallots in this easy recipe.

4 cups (1-inch) cubed peeled butternut squash (about 1½ pounds)
1 tablespoon olive oil
¼ teaspoon salt
4 large shallots, peeled and halved
1 (½-inch) piece peeled fresh ginger, thinly sliced
2½ cups fat-free, lower-sodium chicken broth
2 tablespoons chopped fresh chives
Cracked black pepper (optional)

1. Preheat oven to 375°.
2. Combine first 5 ingredients in a roasting pan or jelly-roll pan; toss well. Bake at 375° for 50 minutes or until tender, stirring occasionally. Cool 10 minutes.
3. Place half of squash mixture and half of broth in a blender. Remove center piece of blender lid (to allow steam to escape); secure blender lid on blender. Place a clean towel over opening in blender lid (to avoid splatters). Blend until smooth. Pour into a large saucepan. Repeat procedure with remaining squash mixture and broth. Cook over medium heat 5 minutes or until thoroughly heated. Top with chives and pepper, if desired. **Yield: 6 servings (serving size: ⅔ cup soup and 1 teaspoon chives).**

CALORIES 112; FAT 2.5g (sat 0.4g, mono 1.7g, poly 0.3g); PROTEIN 3.3g; CARB 22.4g; FIBER 3.6g; CHOL 0mg; IRON 1.6mg; SODIUM 266mg; CALC 84mg

This soup tastes absolutely great, and I think using fresh ginger makes the difference. This is a recipe I will definitely make again for my family, especially on a cold winter night.

—Betty Barfield

Leek and Lima Bean Soup with Bacon

{Check for **Gluten**}

The slightly sweet salad is a nice complement to the smoky-savory soup. Fresh limas are at their peak from June to September; thawed frozen beans are a good substitute for fresh.

3 bacon slices
2 cups chopped leek (about 2 leeks)
4 cups fresh baby lima beans
4 cups fat-free, lower-sodium chicken broth
1 cup water
2 tablespoons fresh lemon juice
½ teaspoon salt
¼ teaspoon freshly ground black pepper
½ cup thinly sliced green onions
½ cup reduced-fat sour cream

1. Cook bacon in a large saucepan over medium heat until crisp. Remove bacon from pan, reserving 1 tablespoon drippings in pan. Crumble bacon; set aside. Add leek to drippings in pan; cook 7 minutes or until tender, stirring frequently. Stir in beans, broth, and 1 cup water; bring to a boil. Reduce heat, and simmer 10 minutes or until beans are tender.

2. Place half of bean mixture in a blender. Remove center piece of blender lid (to allow steam to escape); secure lid on blender. Place a clean towel over opening in blender lid (to avoid splatters), and blend until smooth. Pour pureed bean mixture into a large bowl; repeat procedure with remaining bean mixture. Stir in lemon juice, salt, and pepper. Ladle about 1 cup soup into each of 8 bowls; top each serving with 1 tablespoon onions, 1 tablespoon sour cream, and about 1 teaspoon bacon. **Yield: 8 servings.**

CALORIES 170; FAT 5g (sat 2.4g, mono 1.8g, poly 0.5g); PROTEIN 8.9g; CARB 22.6g; FIBER 6.1g; CHOL 10mg; IRON 2.3mg; SODIUM 440mg; CALC 55mg

Crunchy Chopped Salad:

Combine 6 cups chopped romaine lettuce, 2 cups chopped cucumber, 2 cups sugar snap peas (sliced in half crosswise), 2 cups chopped plum tomato, and 1 cup chopped green onions. Combine ¼ cup cider vinegar, 1½ tablespoons sugar, 1 tablespoon olive oil, and ¾ teaspoon salt; stir with a whisk. Drizzle over salad; toss gently to coat. Sprinkle with 3 tablespoons toasted sliced almonds. **Yield: 8 servings.**

CALORIES 69; FAT 3.1g (sat 0.4g, mono 1.9g, poly 0.6g); PROTEIN 2g; CARB 9g; FIBER 2.8g; CHOL 0mg; IRON 1.2mg; SODIUM 230mg; CALC 45mg

Winter Minestrone

{Check for **Gluten**}

Prep all the vegetables a day ahead, and this soup will come together quickly.

2 teaspoons olive oil
½ cup chopped onion
½ teaspoon dried basil
½ teaspoon dried oregano
2 garlic cloves, minced
1¼ cups cubed peeled acorn or butternut squash (about 1 medium)
¾ cup diced zucchini
½ cup chopped carrot
½ cup diced fennel bulb
1 cup water
1 (14-ounce) can fat-free, lower-sodium chicken broth
5 tablespoons no-salt-added tomato paste
¼ cup uncooked gluten-free tubetini pasta
2½ cups chopped Swiss chard
½ cup rinsed and drained canned Great Northern beans
½ teaspoon freshly ground black pepper
2 tablespoons grated Asiago cheese

1. Heat oil in a Dutch oven over medium-high heat. Add onion and next 3 ingredients to pan; sauté 5 minutes or until onion is tender. Add squash and next 3 ingredients; sauté 5 minutes. Stir in 1 cup water, broth, and tomato paste; bring to a boil. Reduce heat, and simmer 10 minutes or until vegetables are crisp-tender. Stir in pasta; cook 8 minutes, stirring occasionally. Add chard; cook 3 minutes. Add beans; cook 2 minutes or until thoroughly heated. Stir in pepper, and sprinkle with cheese.
Yield: 6 servings (serving size: about 1 cup minestrone and 1 teaspoon cheese).

CALORIES 103; FAT 2.7g (sat 0.7g, mono 1.2g, poly 0.3g); PROTEIN 4.6g; CARB 16.6g; FIBER 4.1g; CHOL 2mg; IRON 1.4mg; SODIUM 288mg; CALC 64mg

Cooking Tip

To easily peel and cube acorn squash, first pierce the shell of the squash in several places with a fork, and microwave at HIGH 2 minutes. Let the squash cool slightly before peeling it, and then use a vegetable peeler to remove the skin. Once you've peeled it, cut the squash in half, scoop out the seeds using a spoon or your fingers, and cube it.

Baked Potato and Bacon Soup

{Check for **Gluten**}

2½ pounds baking potatoes
4 bacon slices
2¼ cups chopped onion
½ teaspoon salt
3 garlic cloves, minced
1 bay leaf
3¾ cups 1% low-fat milk
½ teaspoon black pepper
1½ cups fat-free, lower-sodium chicken broth
2 tablespoons chopped fresh parsley (optional)
½ cup sliced green onions
½ cup (2½ ounces) finely shredded reduced-fat sharp cheddar cheese

1. Preheat oven to 400°.

2. Pierce potatoes with a fork; bake at 400° for 1 hour or until tender. Cool slightly. Partially mash potatoes, including skins, with a potato masher; set aside.

3. Cook bacon in a Dutch oven over medium heat until crisp. Remove bacon from pan; crumble. Add onion to bacon drippings in pan; sauté 5 minutes. Add salt, garlic, and bay leaf; sauté 2 minutes. Add potato, milk, pepper, and broth; bring to a boil. Reduce heat, and simmer 10 minutes. Discard bay leaf. Stir in parsley, if desired. Top individual servings with bacon, green onions, and cheese. **Yield: 9 cups (serving size: 1 cup soup, about 1 teaspoon bacon, about 1 tablespoon cheese, and about 1 tablespoon green onions).**

CALORIES 235; FAT 7.4g (sat 3.3g, mono 2.9g, poly 0.6g); PROTEIN 10.2g; CARB 32g; FIBER 3.6g; CHOL 19mg; IRON 1.2mg; SODIUM 422mg; CALC 213mg

Lentil Soup with Balsamic-Roasted Winter Vegetables

☑ Dairy **free**
{Check for **Gluten**}

1⅔ cups cubed peeled sweet
    potato (about 8 ounces)
1⅔ cups cubed peeled parsnip
    (about 8 ounces)
1⅔ cups cubed peeled carrot
    (about 8 ounces)
 3 tablespoons balsamic vinegar,
    divided
 2 tablespoons olive oil
 ⅛ teaspoon kosher salt
 1 cup (4 ounces) chopped
    pancetta
 1 cup chopped shallots (about
    6 large)
 1 cup chopped red onion (about
    1 medium)
 1 tablespoon fresh thyme leaves
 1 tablespoon minced garlic
 ½ teaspoon black pepper
 ¼ cup dry white wine
1¼ cups dried lentils
 6 cups fat-free, lower-sodium
    chicken broth, divided
 8 cups Swiss chard, trimmed
    and chopped (about 9 ounces)

1. Preheat oven to 375°.

2. Combine sweet potato, parsnip, carrot, 2 tablespoons vinegar, olive oil, and salt in a large bowl; toss well. Arrange vegetable mixture in a single layer on a foil-lined jelly-roll pan; bake at 375° for 30 minutes or until lightly browned, stirring occasionally. Set aside.

3. Cook pancetta in a Dutch oven over medium-high heat 8 minutes or until crisp. Remove from pan with a slotted spoon; set aside. Add shallots and onion to drippings in pan; cook 15 minutes or until golden. Add thyme, garlic, remaining 1 tablespoon vinegar, and pepper, and cook 1 minute. Add wine, scraping pan to loosen browned bits. Add pancetta, lentils, and 4 cups broth to pan; bring to a boil. Cover, reduce heat, and simmer 30 minutes. Add remaining 2 cups broth and roasted vegetables to pan, and simmer, uncovered, 15 minutes. Add chard, and cook 2 minutes or until wilted. **Yield: 6 servings (serving size: about 1½ cups).**

CALORIES 373; FAT 11.7g (sat 3.5g, mono 6.4g, poly 1.6g); PROTEIN 18.8g; CARB 51g; FIBER 15.3g; CHOL 14mg; IRON 6.4mg; SODIUM 875mg; CALC 118mg

Radicchio-Endive Winter Salad:

Combine 3 cups chopped radicchio and 3 cups chopped endive in a large bowl. Combine 2 tablespoons orange juice, 2 teaspoons extra-virgin olive oil, ¼ teaspoon salt, and ⅛ teaspoon freshly ground black pepper in a small bowl; stir with a whisk. Drizzle over salad greens; toss gently to coat. **Yield: 6 servings.**

CALORIES 25; FAT 1.7g (sat 0.2g, mono 1.2g, poly 0.2g); PROTEIN 0.6g; CARB 2.3g; FIBER 1g; CHOL 0mg; IRON 0.3mg; SODIUM 107mg; CALC 18mg

Coconut-Curry Chicken Soup

☑ Dairy **free**

{Check for **Gluten**}

Coconut and curry flavors make this Thai dish a reader favorite. Snow peas, spinach, and chicken breast give the soup flavor, texture, and a wealth of nutrients.

4 cups water
3 cups fresh spinach leaves
½ pound snow peas, trimmed and cut in half crosswise
1 (5¾-ounce) package pad thai noodles (rice stick noodles)
1 tablespoon canola oil
¼ cup thinly sliced shallots
2 teaspoons red curry paste
1½ teaspoons curry powder
½ teaspoon ground turmeric
½ teaspoon ground coriander
2 garlic cloves, minced
6 cups fat-free, lower-sodium chicken broth
1 (13.5-ounce) can light coconut milk
2½ cups shredded cooked chicken breast (about 1 pound)
½ cup chopped green onions
2 tablespoons sugar
2 tablespoons fish sauce (such as Thai Kitchen
½ cup chopped fresh cilantro
4 small hot red chiles, seeded and chopped
7 lime wedges

1. Bring 4 cups water to a boil in a large saucepan. Add spinach and peas to pan; cook 30 seconds. Remove vegetables from pan with a slotted spoon; place in a large bowl. Add noodles to pan; cook 3 minutes. Drain; add noodles to spinach mixture in bowl.

2. Heat canola oil in pan over medium-high heat. Add shallots and next 5 ingredients to pan; sauté 1 minute, stirring constantly. Add chicken broth to pan, and bring to a boil. Add coconut milk to pan; reduce heat, and simmer 5 minutes. Add chicken, onions, sugar, and fish sauce to pan; cook 2 minutes. Pour chicken mixture over noodle mixture in bowl. Stir in cilantro and chiles. Serve with lime wedges. **Yield: 7 servings (serving size: 2 cups soup and 1 lime wedge).**

CALORIES 315; FAT 7.8g (sat 3.7g, mono 2.2g, poly 1.3g); PROTEIN 29.3g; CARB 30.9g; FIBER 2.4g; CHOL 62mg; IRON 3.2mg; SODIUM 841mg; CALC 78mg

Cooking Tip

You can substitute ¼ teaspoon crushed red pepper for the hot red chiles, if you'd like.

Quick Chicken Noodle Soup

☑ Dairy **free**
{Check for **Gluten**}

Heat the broth mixture in the microwave to jump-start the cooking. While the broth mixture heats, sauté the aromatic ingredients in your soup pot to get this dish under way. Though we like the shape of fusilli, you can also make this soup with gluten-free rotini or orzo.

2 cups water
1 (32-ounce) carton fat-free, lower-sodium chicken broth
1 tablespoon olive oil
½ cup chopped onion
½ cup chopped celery
1 medium carrot, chopped
½ teaspoon salt
½ teaspoon freshly ground black pepper
6 ounces gluten-free fusilli (short twisted spaghetti)
2½ cups shredded skinless, boneless rotisserie chicken breast
2 tablespoons chopped fresh flat-leaf parsley

1. Combine 2 cups water and chicken broth in a microwave-safe dish, and microwave at HIGH 5 minutes.

2. While broth mixture heats, heat a large saucepan over medium-high heat. Add oil to pan; swirl to coat. Add onion, celery, carrot, salt, and pepper; sauté 3 minutes or until almost tender. Add hot broth mixture and pasta; bring to a boil. Cook 7 minutes or until pasta is almost al dente. Stir in chicken; cook 1 minute or until thoroughly heated. Stir in parsley. **Yield: 6 servings (serving size: about 1 cup).**

CALORIES 231; FAT 4.9g (sat 0.9g, mono 2.4g, poly 0.7g); PROTEIN 21.7g; CARB 23.6g; FIBER 1.7g; CHOL 50mg; IRON 1.4mg; SODIUM 586mg; CALC 31mg

Fisherman's Seafood Stew

☑ Dairy **free**

This fast-cooking stew is brimming with fish and mussels. Serve with a gluten-free French bread baguette to soak up the broth.

  2 tablespoons olive oil
  ½ cup minced fresh onion or shallots
  ½ cup finely chopped red bell pepper
  ¾ cup dry white wine
  ½ teaspoon salt
  ½ teaspoon dried basil
  ¼ teaspoon black pepper
  2 garlic cloves, minced
  1 (14.5-ounce) can diced tomatoes, undrained
  1 bay leaf
  1 pound grouper or other firm white fish fillets, cut into pieces
1½ pounds small mussels, scrubbed and debearded
  2 tablespoons chopped fresh flat-leaf parsley

1. Heat oil in a large Dutch oven over medium heat. Add onion and bell pepper; cook 5 minutes. Add wine and next 6 ingredients; bring to a boil. Reduce heat; simmer 5 minutes, stirring occasionally.

2. Nestle fish into tomato mixture; top with mussels. Cover and cook 8 minutes; gently shake pan twice to stir mussels (do not lift lid). Discard bay leaf and any unopened shells. Sprinkle with parsley. **Yield: 5 servings (serving size: about 2 ounces fish, ⅔ cup broth mixture, and about 8 mussels).**

CALORIES 284; FAT 9.6g (sat 1.6g, mono 4.9g, poly 1.6g); PROTEIN 35.3g; CARB 13.4g; FIBER 1.4g; CHOL 72mg; IRON 7.3mg; SODIUM 799mg; CALC 102mg

Cooking Tip

It's important to scrub each mussel to remove any sand or dirt on the shell. Just hold it under cool running water, and scrub each shell with a stiff-bristled brush, such as a vegetable brush. Then grab the byssal threads (or beard) with your fingers, and pull them out, tugging toward the hinge of the shell.

Beef Stew

Serve this Mediterranean-inspired stew with mashed potatoes. Make and keep it warm in a Dutch oven or slow cooker.

1½ teaspoons olive oil
1½ pounds beef stew meat, cut into 1-inch pieces
3½ cups halved mushrooms (about 8 ounces)
2 cups diagonally cut carrot
1½ cups coarsely chopped onion
1½ cups sliced celery
2 garlic cloves, minced
1½ cups water
1 cup cabernet sauvignon or other dry red wine
1¼ teaspoons kosher salt
½ teaspoon dried thyme
¼ teaspoon coarsely ground black pepper
2 (14.5-ounce) cans no-salt-added stewed tomatoes, undrained
2 bay leaves
1 (2¼-ounce) can sliced ripe olives, drained
2 tablespoons red wine vinegar
¼ cup chopped fresh flat-leaf parsley

1. Heat oil in a large Dutch oven over medium-high heat. Add beef; cook 5 minutes, browning on all sides. Remove from pan. Add mushrooms and next 4 ingredients to pan; cook 5 minutes, stirring occasionally. Return beef to pan. Stir in 1½ cups water and next 6 ingredients; bring to a boil. Cover, reduce heat, and simmer 1 hour. Stir in olives, and cook 30 minutes or until beef is tender. Discard bay leaves. Stir in vinegar. Sprinkle with parsley.

Yield: 6 servings (serving size: 1⅓ cups).

CALORIES 288; FAT 10.3g (sat 3.3g, mono 5g, poly 0.6g); PROTEIN 25.2g; CARB 20.1g; FIBER 5.7g; CHOL 71mg; IRON 5.5mg; SODIUM 584mg; CALC 100mg

Moroccan Chickpea Chili

☑ Dairy **free**

This recipe comes together quickly and proves you don't need meat to make a hearty chili.

   2 **teaspoons olive oil**
   1 **cup chopped onion**
   ¾ **cup chopped celery**
   ½ **cup chopped carrot**
   1 **teaspoon bottled minced garlic**
   2 **teaspoons ground cumin**
   2 **teaspoons paprika**
   1 **teaspoon ground ginger**
   ½ **teaspoon ground turmeric**
   ¼ **teaspoon salt**
   ¼ **teaspoon freshly ground black pepper**
   ⅛ **teaspoon ground cinnamon**
   ⅛ **teaspoon ground red pepper**
 1½ **cups water**
   2 **tablespoons no-salt-added tomato paste**
   2 **(15½-ounce) cans chickpeas (garbanzo beans), rinsed and drained**
   1 **(14.5-ounce) can no-salt-added diced tomatoes, undrained**
   2 **tablespoons chopped fresh cilantro**
   1 **tablespoon fresh lemon juice**

1. Heat oil in a large saucepan over medium-high heat. Add onion and next 3 ingredients; sauté 5 minutes. Stir in cumin and next 7 ingredients; cook 1 minute, stirring constantly. Add 1½ cups water, tomato paste, chickpeas, and tomatoes; bring to a boil. Cover, reduce heat, and simmer 20 minutes. Stir in cilantro and juice. **Yield: 4 servings (serving size: 1½ cups).**

CALORIES 215; FAT 5.5g (sat 0.4g, mono 2.9g, poly 1.9g); PROTEIN 7.7g; CARB 36.3g; FIBER 9.8g; CHOL 0mg; IRON 3.4mg; SODIUM 534mg; CALC 102mg

Cooking Tip

Bottled minced garlic is a time-saver in the kitchen, but if you have the time, mince your own from fresh garlic cloves for a fresher flavor. One small clove will yield about 1 teaspoon of minced.

Cincinnati Turkey Chili

[Check for **Gluten**]

4 ounces uncooked gluten-free spaghetti
Cooking spray
8 ounces ground turkey breast
1½ cups chopped onion, divided
1 cup chopped green bell pepper
1 tablespoon bottled minced garlic
1 tablespoon chili powder
2 tablespoons tomato paste
1 teaspoon ground cumin
1 teaspoon dried oregano
¼ teaspoon ground cinnamon
⅛ teaspoon ground allspice
½ cup fat-free, lower-sodium chicken broth
1 (15-ounce) can kidney beans, rinsed and drained
1 (14.5-ounce) can diced tomatoes, undrained
2½ tablespoons chopped semisweet chocolate
¼ teaspoon salt
¾ cup (3 ounces) shredded sharp cheddar cheese

1. Cook pasta according to package directions, omitting salt and fat. Drain; set aside.

2. Heat a Dutch oven over medium-high heat. Coat pan with cooking spray. Add turkey; cook 3 minutes, stirring to crumble. Add 1 cup onion, bell pepper, and garlic; sauté 3 minutes. Stir in chili powder and next 5 ingredients; cook 1 minute. Add broth, beans, and tomatoes; bring to a boil. Cover, reduce heat, and simmer 20 minutes, stirring occasionally. Remove from heat; stir in chocolate and salt. Serve chili over spaghetti; top with remaining ½ cup onion and cheese. **Yield: 4 servings (serving size: about ½ cup spaghetti, 1½ cups chili, 2 tablespoons onion, and 3 tablespoons cheese).**

CALORIES 415; FAT 14.5g (sat 6.6g, mono 5g, poly 1.8g); PROTEIN 22.7g; CARB 49.2g; FIBER 9.5g; CHOL 67mg; IRON 4.3mg; SODIUM 797mg; CALC 226mg

Cornbread:

Place an 8-inch cast-iron skillet in oven; preheat oven to 425°. Weigh or lightly spoon 1.1 ounces gluten-free all-purpose flour (about ¼ cup; such as Bob's Red Mill) into a dry measuring cup; level with a knife. Combine flour, 1 cup cornmeal (such as Bob's Red Mill), 1 tablespoon sugar, 1¼ teaspoons baking powder, and ½ teaspoon salt in a medium bowl. Combine ¾ cup low-fat buttermilk, 1 tablespoon olive oil, and 1 large egg in a separate bowl, stirring with a whisk until blended. Make a well in center of cornmeal mixture; add buttermilk mixture, stirring just until moist. Remove skillet from oven, and coat well with cooking spray. Spoon batter into prepared pan. Bake at 425° for 20 minutes or until lightly browned. Remove skillet from oven; invert cornbread onto a plate. Cut into wedges, and serve immediately. **Yield: 8 servings (serving size: 1 wedge).**

CALORIES 108; FAT 3.3g (sat 0.6g, mono 1.5g, poly 0.3g); PROTEIN 2.9g; CARB 17.1g; FIBER 1.4g; CHOL 27mg; IRON 0.7mg; SODIUM 246mg; CALC 75mg

Desserts

Chewy Gooey Marshmallow Cookies with Minichips

{Check for **Gluten**}

2 large eggs
½ cup canola oil
2 tablespoons water
1 (20-ounce) package gluten-free cookie mix (such as Namaste)
1 teaspoon ground cinnamon
⅛ teaspoon ground nutmeg
⅔ cup miniature marshmallows
¼ cup semisweet chocolate minichips
¼ cup sweetened dried cranberries
¼ cup coarsely chopped pecans, toasted

1. Preheat oven to 350°.

2. Beat first 3 ingredients with a mixer at medium speed until blended. Add cookie mix, cinnamon, and nutmeg; beat until blended. Stir in marshmallows and remaining 3 ingredients.

3. Drop dough by level tablespoons 2 inches apart onto baking sheets lined with parchment paper.

4. Bake at 350° for 12 minutes or until lightly browned. **Yield: 54 servings (serving size: 1 cookie).**

CALORIES 69; FAT 2.9g (sat 0.4g, mono 1.7g, poly 0.7g); PROTEIN 0.8g; CARB 10.7g; FIBER 0.6g; CHOL 8mg; IRON 0.1mg; SODIUM 51mg; CALC 2mg

Cooking Tip

Toasting the pecans gives them a nuttier flavor. Spread the pecans on a baking sheet, and toast them in a 350° oven for 6 to 8 minutes; or place them in a dry skillet, and cook over medium heat 1 to 2 minutes, stirring frequently, until they're toasted. Whichever toasting method you choose, watch the pecans carefully—they can go from toasted to burned quickly.

Piña Colada Cheesecake Bars

This recipe uses a small amount of coconut flour, which is slightly sweet, high in fiber (3 grams per tablespoon), and gluten free. Look for it in health-food stores or order online. You also can substitute an equal amount of gluten-free all-purpose flour.

1 cup gluten-free graham cracker crumbs
2 tablespoons coconut flour
2 tablespoons turbinado sugar
½ teaspoon ground ginger
2 tablespoons butter, melted
1 tablespoon canola oil
1 tablespoon water
Cooking spray
1 cup 2% low-fat cottage cheese
½ cup sugar
¼ cup (2 ounces) block-style fat-free cream cheese, softened
1½ tablespoons grated lemon rind
1 tablespoon fresh lemon juice
1 tablespoon pineapple juice
½ teaspoon vanilla extract
Dash of salt
¾ cup egg substitute
1 cup chopped fresh pineapple
¼ cup shredded unsweetened coconut, toasted

1. Preheat oven to 350°.

2. Combine first 4 ingredients in a bowl. Add butter, oil, and 1 tablespoon water; toss well. Press mixture into bottom of an 8-inch square metal baking pan coated with cooking spray. Bake at 350° for 10 minutes. Cool completely on a wire rack.

3. Place cottage cheese and next 7 ingredients in a food processor; process until smooth. Add egg substitute, and process until blended. Spread cheese mixture over cooled crust. Bake at 350° for 33 minutes or until set. Cool 10 minutes on a wire rack. Refrigerate 2 hours or until thoroughly chilled. Top with pineapple and coconut. Cut into 16 bars. **Yield: 16 servings (serving size: 1 bar).**

CALORIES 117; FAT 4.6g (sat 2.2g, mono 1.2g, poly 0.7g); PROTEIN 4.1g; CARB 15.4g; FIBER 0.9g; CHOL 6mg; IRON 0.5mg; SODIUM 142mg; CALC 27mg

Cooking Tip

Standard lemons work well in this recipe, but Meyer lemons, which have a sweeter flavor, are a delicious substitute if you can find them in good condition. Often, you'll find lemons that are too soft, or dry and shriveled. Avoid these. What you want are plump, shiny-skinned fruits that are firm but not hard and seemingly heavy for their size, which is a good sign that they're full of juice.

Fresh Ginger Cereal Squares

Be sure to add the fresh ginger to the melted marshmallows to get the best distribution of its delicious pungent flavor.

Cooking spray
2 tablespoons butter
4 cups miniature marshmallows
2 teaspoons grated peeled fresh ginger
4 cups gluten-free flax, corn, and amaranth multigrain cereal (such as Nature's Path)
½ cup sliced almonds, toasted
⅓ cup dried apricots, chopped
⅓ cup sweetened dried cranberries

1. Coat a 9-inch square metal baking pan with cooking spray.
2. Melt butter in a 4-quart Dutch oven over medium heat. Add marshmallows. Cook 4 minutes or until marshmallows melt, stirring frequently; stir in ginger. Stir in cereal, nuts, and dried fruit. Gently press mixture into prepared pan using wax paper to prevent mixture from sticking to hands. Cool completely; cut into 16 squares. **Yield: 16 servings (serving size: 1 square).**

CALORIES 117; FAT 3.3g (sat 1g, mono 1.4g, poly 0.6g); PROTEIN 2.3g; CARB 22.3g; FIBER 2.7g; CHOL 4mg; IRON 0.8mg; SODIUM 66mg; CALC 10mg

Cooking Tip

Cooking sprays marked specifically for baking contain flour and should be avoided. Just use regular gluten-free cooking spray instead.

Easy Chocolate-Caramel Brownies

{Check for **Gluten**}

Cut the brownies after they've cooled to get a clean edge. To make ahead, cool the brownies completely, wrap them tightly in heavy-duty plastic wrap, and freeze.

 2 tablespoons fat-free milk
27 small soft caramel candies
    (about 8 ounces)
 ½ cup fat-free sweetened
    condensed milk (not
    evaporated fat-free milk)
 1 (15-ounce) package gluten-free
    devil's food cake mix (such as
    Betty Crocker)
 7 tablespoons butter, melted
 1 large egg white, lightly beaten
Cooking spray
 1 teaspoon gluten-free
    all-purpose flour (such as
    Bob's Red Mill)
 ½ cup chocolate baking chips

1. Preheat oven to 350°.

2. Combine fat-free milk and candies in a bowl. Microwave at HIGH 1½ to 2 minutes or until caramels melt and mixture is smooth, stirring with a whisk after every minute. Set aside.

3. Combine sweetened condensed milk, cake mix, butter, and egg white in a bowl; stir well (batter will be very stiff). Coat bottom only of a 13 x 9–inch metal baking pan with cooking spray; dust lightly with flour. Press two-thirds of batter into prepared pan using floured hands; pat evenly (layer will be thin).

4. Bake at 350° for 10 minutes. Remove from oven; sprinkle with chocolate chips. Drizzle caramel mixture over chips; carefully drop remaining batter by spoonfuls over caramel mixture. Bake at 350° for 25 minutes or until done. Cool completely in pan on a wire rack. **Yield: 36 brownies (serving size: 1 brownie).**

CALORIES 131; FAT 3.8g (sat 2.2g, mono 1g, poly 0.4g); PROTEIN 1.4g; CARB 23.5g; FIBER 0.2g; CHOL 7mg; IRON 0mg; SODIUM 41mg; CALC 23mg

Mocha Cream Brownie Wedges with Fresh Raspberries

You'd never guess by looking at this sophisticated dessert that it started from a boxed brownie mix.

4 large egg whites
1 (16-ounce) package gluten-free brownie mix (such as Betty Crocker)
6 tablespoons canola oil
1 tablespoon instant coffee granules
Cooking spray
1 cup heavy whipping cream
2 teaspoons instant coffee granules
½ teaspoon vanilla extract
¼ cup powdered sugar
½ cup chocolate syrup
1½ cups raspberries

1. Preheat oven to 350°.

2. Beat egg whites with a mixer at high speed for 1 minute or until frothy. Stir in brownie mix, oil, and 1 tablespoon coffee granules. (Batter will be very thick.) Spread batter in an 11 x 7–inch glass or ceramic baking dish coated with cooking spray.

3. Bake at 350° for 22 minutes or until a wooden pick inserted 2 inches from edge comes out clean. (Center will not look cooked, but will continue to cook as brownies cool.) Cool completely in dish on a wire rack. Cut into 6 squares; cut each square diagonally in half to create 12 triangles.

4. Place cream, 2 teaspoons coffee granules, and vanilla in a medium bowl; beat with a mixer at high speed until foamy. Add powdered sugar; beat until soft peaks form.

5. Place 1 brownie on each of 12 dessert plates. Drizzle evenly with chocolate syrup. Dollop evenly with topping, and sprinkle evenly with raspberries. **Yield: 12 servings (serving size: 1 brownie, 2 teaspoons chocolate syrup, and 2 tablespoons raspberries).**

CALORIES 338; FAT 17.3g (sat 6.5g, mono 6.6g, poly 2.3g); PROTEIN 3.5g; CARB 45.9g; FIBER 2.4g; CHOL 27mg; IRON 1.4mg; SODIUM 107mg; CALC 18mg

The brownie is to die for! It was very easy to prepare, and I love the mocha taste from the instant coffee. I substituted strawberries for the raspberries.

—Barbara Wallace

Carrot Cake

This deliciously moist cake is chock-full of carrots, nuts, and raisins.

Cake:
- 2 teaspoons ground cinnamon
- 1 teaspoon grated orange rind
- ⅔ cup fresh orange juice
- ½ cup vegetable oil
- 4 large eggs
- 1 (15-ounce) package gluten-free yellow cake mix (such as Betty Crocker)
- 1 (3.4-ounce) package gluten-free vanilla instant pudding mix
- 3⅓ cups grated carrot (about 1 pound carrots)
- ¾ cup raisins
- ¾ cup chopped walnuts
- Cooking spray

Frosting:
- 6 ounces ⅓-less-fat cream cheese, softened
- 2 tablespoons 1% low-fat milk
- 1½ teaspoons vanilla extract
- 4½ cups powdered sugar, sifted

1. Preheat oven to 350°.

2. To prepare cake, combine first 7 ingredients in a bowl; beat with a mixer at low speed for 1 minute. Scrape sides of bowl; beat at medium-high speed for 2 minutes or until batter is smooth, scraping sides of bowl occasionally. (Batter will be thick.) Fold in carrot, raisins, and walnuts. Spoon batter evenly into 2 (9-inch) round cake pans coated with cooking spray.

3. Bake at 350° for 30 minutes or until a wooden pick inserted in center comes out clean. Cool in pans 10 minutes; remove from pans. Cool completely on a wire rack.

4. To prepare frosting, place cream cheese, milk, and vanilla in a large bowl; beat with a mixer at high speed until creamy. Gradually add powdered sugar; beat at low speed just until blended.

5. Place 1 cake layer on a plate; spread with ½ cup frosting. Top with remaining cake layer. Spread remaining frosting over top and sides of cake. **Yield: 22 servings (serving size: 1 slice).**

CALORIES 332; FAT 10.4g (sat 2.2g, mono 2.9g, poly 4.2g); PROTEIN 3.2g; CARB 59.4g; FIBER 1.1g; CHOL 44mg; IRON 0.5mg; SODIUM 119mg; CALC 28mg

Chocolate Layer Cake

{Check for **Gluten**}

This stunning dessert is also delicious using unsweetened almond milk in both the cake and frosting.

Cake:
- 1¾ cups 1% low-fat milk, divided
- 1 cup semisweet chocolate chips
- 3.3 ounces brown rice flour (about ¾ cup; such as Bob's Red Mill)
- 4.35 ounces potato starch (about ¾ cup)
- 2.1 ounces tapioca flour (about ½ cup)
- 2 teaspoons baking powder
- 1 teaspoon xanthan gum (such as Bob's Red Mill)
- ½ teaspoon baking soda
- ½ teaspoon salt
- 2 large eggs
- 1 cup granulated sugar
- ½ cup canola oil
- 1 tablespoon vanilla extract
- Cooking spray

Frosting:
- 6 cups sifted powdered sugar
- ¾ cup unsweetened cocoa
- 5 tablespoons 1% low-fat milk
- 1 tablespoon vanilla extract
- ½ cup light butter, softened
- ¼ cup raspberries (optional)
- 3 mint sprigs (optional)

1. Preheat oven to 350°.
2. To prepare cake, heat ¾ cup milk in a small saucepan over medium-low heat 2 minutes or until warm; add chocolate chips, stirring until smooth. Cool.
3. Weigh or lightly spoon brown rice flour, potato starch, and tapioca flour into dry measuring cups; level with a knife. Combine flours and next 4 ingredients in a bowl; stir with a whisk.
4. Combine eggs and next 3 ingredients in a bowl; beat with a mixer at low speed until blended. Add chocolate mixture, beating until blended. Add flour mixture alternately with remaining 1 cup milk, beginning and ending with dry ingredients; beat until smooth. Pour batter evenly into 2 (9-inch) round cake pans coated with cooking spray and lined with parchment paper.
5. Bake at 350° for 25 minutes or until a wooden pick inserted in center comes out clean. Cool in pans 10 minutes; remove from pans. Cool completely on a wire rack.
6. To prepare frosting, combine powdered sugar and cocoa in a large bowl; stir with a whisk. Combine milk and vanilla. Place butter in a separate bowl; beat with a mixer at medium speed until creamy. Add powdered sugar mixture alternately with milk mixture, beating well after each addition until spreading consistency.
7. Place 1 cake layer on a plate; spread with 1 cup frosting. Top with remaining cake layer. Spread remaining frosting over top and sides of cake. Garnish with raspberries and mint sprigs, if desired. **Yield: 22 servings (serving size: 1 slice).**

CALORIES 332; FAT 10.8g (sat 3.6g, mono 4.4g, poly 1.7g); PROTEIN 2.6g; CARB 60.5g; FIBER 1.7g; CHOL 26mg; IRON 0.9mg; SODIUM 180mg; CALC 61mg

Somebody get me a glass of milk!

I almost forgot what chocolate cake tastes like—thanks for the reminder. Although a lot of gluten-free desserts turn out dry, this cake was very moist. The icing was definitely the "icing on the cake"! Very rich and the perfect complement to the cake.

—*Roxanne D. Osborne*

Orange-Scented Shortcakes with Mango and Berries

Fresh in-season berries, such as strawberries, raspberries, or blueberries, complement the sweet tropical essence of mango in these delicious shortcakes.

Shortcakes:
2.5 ounces gluten-free biscuit and baking mix (about ¾ cup; such as Bob's Red Mill)
2 tablespoons sugar
1 teaspoon ground cinnamon
2 egg whites
½ cup low-fat buttermilk
1 teaspoon grated orange rind
½ teaspoon vanilla extract

Topping:
½ teaspoon grated orange rind
½ cup orange juice
1 tablespoon sugar
1 teaspoon vanilla extract
1½ cups (½-inch) cubed mango
1 cup quartered mixed berries
1 cup plain 2% reduced-fat Greek yogurt (optional)

1. Preheat oven to 375°.

2. To prepare shortcakes, line a baking sheet with parchment paper, and set aside.

3. Weigh or lightly spoon baking mix into a dry measuring cup; level with a knife. Combine baking mix, 2 tablespoons sugar, and cinnamon in a medium bowl, stirring with a whisk. Make a well in center of mixture. Place egg whites in a small bowl; stir with a whisk. Add buttermilk, 1 teaspoon orange rind, and ½ teaspoon vanilla, stirring with a whisk. Add to baking mix mixture, stirring just until moist. Spoon batter into 4 mounds 2 inches apart on prepared baking sheet.

4. Bake at 375° for 13 minutes or until golden.

5. To prepare topping, while shortcakes bake, combine ½ teaspoon orange rind and next 3 ingredients in a medium bowl. Add mango and berries, stirring gently to coat.

6. Cut shortcakes in half horizontally using a serrated knife. Place 1 shortcake bottom in each of 4 shallow bowls. Spoon about ½ cup mango mixture and ¼ cup yogurt, if desired, over each shortcake bottom. Top with shortcake tops. **Yield: 4 servings (serving size: 1 shortcake).**

CALORIES 193; FAT 1.1g (sat 0.2g, mono 0.3g, poly 0.3g); PROTEIN 5.6g; CARB 40.9g; FIBER 3.4g; CHOL 1mg; IRON 1.1mg; SODIUM 225mg; CALC 109mg

Strawberry-Chocolate Trifle

1 (15-ounce) package gluten-free devil's food cake mix (such as Betty Crocker)
½ cup unsalted butter, softened
3 large eggs
1 cup water
Cooking spray
2½ cups 1% low-fat milk
1 (1-ounce) package gluten-free vanilla instant pudding mix
1½ (8-ounce) containers frozen reduced-calorie whipped topping, thawed and divided
¼ cup Chambord (raspberry-flavored liqueur; optional)
3 cups strawberries, sliced
2 tablespoons chocolate syrup

1. Preheat oven to 350°.
2. Prepare cake mix according to package directions, using unsalted butter, eggs, and 1 cup water. Pour batter into an 8-inch square metal baking pan coated with cooking spray.
3. Bake at 350° for 38 minutes or until a wooden pick inserted in center comes out clean. Cool in pan 10 minutes. Remove from pan; cool completely on a wire rack.
4. Combine milk and pudding mix in a medium bowl, stirring with a whisk 2 minutes. Cover and chill 5 minutes. Fold in 1 container whipped topping.
5. Cut cake into 1-inch squares. Layer half of cake in bottom of a 4-quart trifle bowl. Brush cake with 2 tablespoons liqueur, if desired; spread half of pudding mixture over cake. Layer half of strawberries over pudding. Reserve ¼ cup of remaining whipped topping. Top strawberries with remaining 1¼ cups whipped topping. Repeat layers with remaining cake, liqueur, if desired, pudding mixture, and strawberries. Cover and chill 8 hours. Dollop center of trifle with reserved ¼ cup whipped topping, and drizzle with chocolate syrup just before serving. **Yield: 16 servings (serving size: 1 cup).**

CALORIES 248; FAT 9.6g (sat 6.6g, mono 2g, poly 0.4g); PROTEIN 3.5g; CARB 38.4g; FIBER 0.6g; CHOL 57mg; IRON 0.3mg; SODIUM 46mg; CALC 57mg

Cooking Tip

You can also serve this trifle in individual glasses. You may need to cut the 1-inch cubes of cake into smaller pieces, and then just layer in the ingredients, creating two layers. Top each with a dollop of whipped topping; drizzle with chocolate sauce.

Chocolate-Cherry Pudding Cake

As the cake bakes, it separates into two layers, a tender chocolate spongelike cake and a rich chocolate-cherry sauce.

1 cup packed light brown sugar
⅓ cup unsweetened cocoa
2 cups hot water
8.6 ounces gluten-free baking and pancake mix (about 2 cups; such as Pamela's)
1 cup granulated sugar
¼ cup unsweetened cocoa
¼ teaspoon salt
¼ cup grapeseed oil
2 teaspoons vanilla extract
½ teaspoon instant espresso granules or 1 teaspoon instant coffee granules
2 large eggs
1 (20-ounce) can light cherry pie filling

1. Preheat oven to 350°.

2. Combine brown sugar, ⅓ cup cocoa, and 2 cups hot water in an ungreased 11 x 7–inch glass or ceramic baking dish, stirring until sugar dissolves.

3. Weigh or lightly spoon baking mix into dry measuring cups; level with a knife. Combine baking mix and next 3 ingredients in a large bowl, stirring with a whisk. Add oil and next 4 ingredients, stirring just until combined.

4. Spoon batter over brown sugar mixture in dish. Set dish on a jelly-roll pan. Bake at 350° for 55 minutes or until cake springs back when touched lightly in center. Cool 30 minutes. Spoon cake and sauce into serving dishes. **Yield: 16 servings (serving size: ¹⁄₁₆ of cake with sauce).**

CALORIES 250; FAT 5.8g (sat 1g, mono 1.4g, poly 2.9g); PROTEIN 3.1g; CARB 48.2g; FIBER 1.8g; CHOL 28mg; IRON 0.9mg; SODIUM 204mg; CALC 61mg

Apple-Cranberry Crisp

Use other apple varieties, such as Jonagold, Honeycrisp, or Melrose, to change the flavor of this crisp.

2 tablespoons granulated sugar
1 tablespoon cornstarch
1 teaspoon ground cinnamon
¼ teaspoon grated whole
   nutmeg
½ cup apple juice
1 tablespoon fresh lemon juice
½ cup sweetened dried
   cranberries
5 medium Braeburn apples
Cooking spray
2.15 ounces gluten-free baking and
   pancake mix (about ½ cup;
   such as Pamela's)
1½ cups gluten-free old-fashioned
   rolled oats (such as Bob's Red
   Mill)
½ cup packed light brown sugar
¼ teaspoon salt
¼ cup unsalted butter, melted

1. Preheat oven to 375°.
2. Combine first 4 ingredients in a large bowl, stirring with a whisk. Gradually add juices, stirring with a whisk until cornstarch dissolves. Add cranberries; let stand while preparing apples.
3. Peel, core, and cut apples into ¼-inch slices to measure 9 cups. Add apples to cranberry mixture, stirring to coat. Pour apple mixture into a 13 x 9–inch glass or ceramic baking dish coated with cooking spray.
4. Weigh or lightly spoon baking mix into a dry measuring cup; level with a knife. Combine baking mix and next 3 ingredients in a medium bowl. Add butter, tossing with a fork until crumbly. Sprinkle oat mixture over apple mixture. Cover with foil.
5. Bake at 375° for 40 minutes. Uncover and bake an additional 15 minutes or until filling is bubbly and topping is brown and crisp. Cool on a wire rack 15 minutes. Serve warm. **Yield: 8 servings (serving size: ⅛ of crisp).**

CALORIES 276; FAT 8.1g (sat 4g, mono 2.2g, poly 1g); PROTEIN 3.7g; CARB 49.1g; FIBER 3.9g; CHOL 16mg; IRON 1mg; SODIUM 151mg; CALC 45mg

The Apple-Cranberry Crisp was a big hit!
I took it to a family function, and no one knew it was gluten free. I had one small bowl left over! The prep took a little while, but it was very tasty and worth the effort!

—Connie Hendon

Cheesecake Pie with Berries

This is a great dish for entertaining because it can be made ahead and topped with berries just prior to serving.

1½ cups pecan halves
 ¼ teaspoon salt
 5 tablespoons sugar, divided
 3 tablespoons unsalted butter, melted
    Cooking spray
 1 (8-ounce) block ⅓-less-fat cream cheese, softened
 1 teaspoon vanilla extract
 1 teaspoon grated lemon rind
 1 tablespoon fresh lemon juice
 1 (12-ounce) container frozen fat-free whipped topping, thawed
 2 cups sliced strawberries

1. Preheat oven to 350°.

2. Place pecans, salt, and 1 tablespoon sugar in a food processor; pulse 15 times or until mixture resembles coarse meal. Add butter; pulse 5 times or until combined. Pat mixture into bottom and up sides of a 9-inch pie plate coated with cooking spray.

3. Bake at 350° for 15 minutes or until lightly browned. Cool crust completely in dish on a wire rack.

4. Beat cream cheese, remaining ¼ cup sugar, and vanilla with a mixer at medium speed until smooth. Add lemon rind and lemon juice; beat well. Fold in one-fourth of whipped topping. Fold in remaining topping. Spoon filling into prepared crust. Cover with plastic wrap, and freeze 8 hours or until firm.

5. Let pie stand at room temperature 10 minutes before serving. Cut into wedges, and top with berries. **Yield: 9 servings (serving size: 1 wedge and about ¼ cup strawberries).**

CALORIES 316; FAT 21.3g (sat 7.1g, mono 7.7g, poly 3.8g); PROTEIN 3.6g; CARB 26.8g; FIBER 2.4g; CHOL 28mg; IRON 0.6mg; SODIUM 186mg; CALC 37mg

Cooking Tip

We opted to use ⅓-less-fat cream cheese over a fat-free variety because the extra fat made the texture smoother and creamier.

Chocolate-Hazelnut Meringues

Make up to two days ahead, and store in an airtight container at room temperature. The chocolate and hazelnut coating adds textural interest to these airy, sweet treats.

  5 **large egg whites**
  ½ **teaspoon cream of tartar**
  ⅛ **teaspoon salt**
  ½ **cup granulated sugar**
  ½ **cup packed brown sugar**
  1 **teaspoon vanilla extract**
  3 ounces semisweet chocolate
  ⅓ **cup blanched whole hazelnuts, toasted and finely chopped**

1. Preheat oven to 250°.

2. Place egg whites in a large bowl; beat with a mixer at high speed until foamy. Add cream of tartar and salt, beating until soft peaks form. Gradually add sugars, 1 tablespoon at a time, beating until stiff peaks form. Add vanilla; beat 1 minute.

3. Cover 2 baking sheets with parchment paper. Spoon 24 (2-inch-round) mounds onto prepared baking sheets. Place in oven; bake at 250° for 1 hour or until dry to touch, rotating pans halfway through cooking. (Meringues are done when surface is dry, and meringues can be removed from paper without sticking to fingers.) Turn oven off. Cool meringues in closed oven 1 hour. Remove from oven; carefully remove meringues from paper.

4. Place chocolate in a medium glass bowl. Microwave at HIGH 1 minute or until almost melted, stirring until smooth. Dip side of each meringue in melted chocolate and chopped hazelnuts.

Yield: 12 servings (serving size: 2 meringues).

CALORIES 135; FAT 4.3g (sat 1.4g, mono 1.7g, poly 0.3g); PROTEIN 2.6g; CARB 22.7g; FIBER 0.4g; CHOL 0mg; IRON 0.6mg; SODIUM 51mg; CALC 13mg

Coconut Pavlovas with Tropical Fruits and Ice Cream

2 cups (1-inch) cubed fresh pineapple
1 cup orange sections
1 cup cubed peeled mango
⅓ cup dried sweet cherries
2 tablespoons sugar
2 tablespoons white rum
⅛ teaspoon ground cinnamon
3 egg whites
¼ teaspoon cream of tartar
¼ teaspoon almond extract
⅔ cup sugar
½ cup flaked sweetened coconut, toasted
1½ cups vanilla light ice cream (optional)
Mint sprigs (optional)

1. Preheat oven to 250°.

2. Combine first 7 ingredients in a bowl; stir well, and set aside. Place parchment paper over a large baking sheet. Draw 6 (4-inch) circles on parchment paper. Turn parchment paper over, and secure with masking tape.

3. Beat egg whites and cream of tartar with a mixer at high speed until foamy. Add extract; beat well. Gradually add ⅔ cup sugar, 1 tablespoon at a time, beating until stiff peaks form. Fold coconut into egg white mixture. Divide egg white mixture evenly among the 6 drawn circles. Shape meringues into nests with 1-inch sides using the back of a spoon.

4. Bake at 250° for 1 hour or until dry. Turn oven off; cool meringue nests in closed oven at least 4 hours. Carefully remove meringue nests from paper.

5. Spoon ¼ cup ice cream, if desired, into each meringue nest, and top with about ⅔ cup fruit mixture. Garnish with mint sprigs, if desired. **Yield: 6 servings.**

CALORIES 236; FAT 2.2g (sat 1.9g, mono 0.1g, poly 0.1g); PROTEIN 3.2g; CARB 51.7g; FIBER 3.4g; CHOL 0mg; IRON 0.4mg; CALC 29mg; SODIUM 50mg

Cooking Tip

Make a template to ensure your pavlovas come out looking perfect. Trace circles onto parchment paper as a guide for shaping the nests; a standard oatmeal can is the perfect size. Turn the paper (and the pencil markings) over before securing to the baking sheet.

Grand Marnier Meringue Torte

{Check for **Gluten**}

This grown-up birthday cake blends delicately crisp meringues, orange-scented cream, a hint of chocolate, and fresh fruit. If you can find a clear vanilla extract, you can use that in this recipe to make the meringues whiter and brighter. Prepare the meringues up to three days ahead, and store at room temperature in an airtight container. Top with filling and fruit shortly before serving.

Meringues:
- 2 teaspoons vanilla extract
- ½ teaspoon cream of tartar
- ⅛ teaspoon salt
- 6 large egg whites
- ¾ cup superfine sugar

Filling:
- 3 cups frozen whipped topping, thawed
- 2 tablespoons Grand Marnier (orange-flavored liqueur)
- 1½ teaspoons finely grated orange rind
- 2 tablespoons grated semisweet chocolate, divided
- ½ cup halved strawberries
- ½ cup blueberries
- ½ cup blackberries
- ½ cup raspberries
- Mint sprigs (optional)
- Orange rind strips (optional)

1. Preheat oven to 200°.

2. To prepare meringues, cover a baking sheet with parchment paper. Draw 3 (8-inch) circles on parchment paper. Turn parchment paper over, and secure with masking tape.

3. Place first 4 ingredients in a large bowl, and beat with a mixer at high speed until foamy. Gradually add sugar, 1 tablespoon at a time, beating until stiff peaks form. Divide egg white mixture evenly among the 3 drawn circles on baking sheet. Spread mixture onto circles using the back of a spoon. Bake at 200° for 2 hours or until dry. Turn oven off; cool meringues in closed oven at least 1 hour. Carefully remove meringues from paper.

4. To prepare filling, combine whipped topping, liqueur, and 1½ teaspoons rind. Place 1 meringue on a serving platter; top with 1 cup whipped topping mixture and 2 teaspoons chocolate. Repeat layers twice with remaining meringues, whipped topping mixture, and chocolate. Combine berries; arrange over torte. Garnish with mint and rind strips, if desired. **Yield: 8 servings (serving size: 1 piece).**

CALORIES 206; FAT 7g (sat 6.5g, mono 0.3g, poly 0.1g); PROTEIN 3.2g; CARB 32.4g; FIBER 1.1g; CHOL 0mg; IRON 0.3mg; SODIUM 95mg; CALC 7mg

Cooking Tip

Superfine sugar dissolves quickly into the beaten egg whites; if you can't find superfine sugar in your grocery store, make your own by processing granulated sugar in a food processor for about a minute.

Almond Crème Caramel

½ cup sugar
4 large eggs
1 teaspoon vanilla extract
½ teaspoon almond extract
1 (14-ounce) can fat-free sweetened condensed milk
1 (12-ounce) can evaporated fat-free milk
¼ cup coarsely chopped almonds
Sliced almonds, toasted (optional)

1. Preheat oven to 350°.
2. Pour sugar into a 9-inch round cake pan. Place cake pan over medium heat. Cook 6 minutes or until sugar dissolves and is golden, shaking cake pan occasionally with tongs. Immediately remove from heat; set aside.
3. Place eggs in a medium bowl; stir with a whisk until foamy. Add extracts and milks; stir with a whisk. Stir in ¼ cup almonds. Pour mixture into prepared cake pan. Cover with foil; place in a large shallow roasting pan. Place roasting pan in oven; add hot water to roasting pan to a depth of 1 inch. Bake at 350° for 55 minutes or until a knife inserted in center comes out clean.
4. Remove cake pan from water; place on a wire rack. Remove foil. Cool custard in cake pan 30 minutes. Loosen edges with a knife or rubber spatula. Place a serving plate upside down on top of cake pan; invert custard onto plate, allowing syrup to drizzle over custard. Sprinkle with sliced almonds, if desired.

Yield: 9 servings (serving size: 1 slice).

CALORIES 253; FAT 4.3g (sat 0.9g, mono 2.1g, poly 0.7g); PROTEIN 9.8g; CARB 43.1g; FIBER 0.4g; CHOL 100mg; IRON 0.6mg; SODIUM 118mg; CALC 131mg

Pumpkin-Praline Custards

☑ Dairy **free**

Substituting soy milk for dairy milk in custards and puddings is a tasty way to increase beneficial soy protein in your diet. A crunchy topping of crumbled praline adds a festive touch to this homey dessert, but it's just as good without it.

1½ cups vanilla soy milk
¾ cup canned pumpkin
⅔ cup sugar
1½ teaspoons ground cinnamon
½ teaspoon ground nutmeg
½ teaspoon vanilla extract
¼ teaspoon salt
2 large eggs
2 large egg whites
  Cooking spray
¼ cup sugar
2 tablespoons water
¼ cup chopped pecans

1. Preheat oven to 325°.

2. Combine first 9 ingredients in a bowl; stir well with a whisk. Divide pumpkin mixture evenly among 6 (6-ounce) custard cups coated with cooking spray. Place cups in a 13 x 9–inch metal baking pan; add hot water to pan to a depth of 1 inch. Bake at 325° for 50 minutes or until a knife inserted in center comes out clean. Remove the cups from pan; cool completely on a wire rack. Cover and chill at least 3 hours.

3. Combine ¼ cup sugar and 2 tablespoons water in a small skillet. Cook over medium-high heat 4 minutes or until golden, stirring occasionally. Remove from heat, and stir in pecans. Immediately scrape pecan mixture onto a baking sheet coated with cooking spray, spreading evenly; cool completely. Break praline into small pieces. Sprinkle over custards. **Yield: 6 servings (serving size: 1 custard and about 1 tablespoon praline).**

CALORIES 220; FAT 6.2g (sat 0.9g, mono 2.9g, poly 1.7g); PROTEIN 5.7g; CARB 37g; FIBER 1.7g; CHOL 71mg; IRON 1mg; SODIUM 235mg; CALC 101mg

Lemon Cloud with Strawberry-Mint Compote

☑ Dairy **free**

This is a case where you want your soufflé to fall. As it does, the lemon flavor intensifies, and the texture becomes almost cakelike. Any berries will work in place of the strawberries.

Cloud:
  Cooking spray
  ¾ cup plus 2 tablespoons sugar, divided
  1 tablespoon cornstarch
  1 tablespoon grated lemon rind
  6 tablespoons fresh lemon juice
  2 large egg yolks
  4 large egg whites
  Dash of salt
Compote:
  2 cups quartered small strawberries
  2 tablespoons sugar
  1 to 2 tablespoons chopped fresh mint

1. To prepare cloud, preheat oven to 350°.

2. Lightly coat a 1½-quart soufflé dish with cooking spray. Sprinkle with 2 tablespoons sugar, shaking out excess. Place dish on a baking sheet.

3. Combine ½ cup sugar and cornstarch in a medium saucepan, stirring with a whisk. Stir in lemon rind, juice, and egg yolks. Place over medium heat; cook 3 minutes or until thick, stirring constantly. Remove from heat; immediately scrape mixture into a glass bowl. Cool to room temperature.

4. Place egg whites and salt in a large bowl; beat with a mixer at medium speed for 30 seconds or until foamy. Increase mixer speed to high. Gradually add remaining ¼ cup sugar, 1 tablespoon at a time, beating just until stiff peaks form. Gently stir one-fourth of egg white mixture into egg yolk mixture; gently fold in remaining egg white mixture. Spoon into prepared dish. Bake at 350° for 25 minutes or until puffy and lightly browned. Remove from oven, and cool to room temperature on a wire rack. Cover and chill.

5. To prepare compote, combine strawberries, 2 tablespoons sugar, and mint; toss gently. Cover and chill. Serve with lemon cloud. **Yield: 6 servings (serving size: ⅙ of cloud and ⅓ cup compote).**

CALORIES 187; FAT 1.9g (sat 0.5g, mono 0.7g, poly 0.3g); PROTEIN 3.8g; CARB 40g; FIBER 1.6g; CHOL 71mg; IRON 0.7mg; SODIUM 65mg; CALC 23mg

Cinnamon Rice Pudding with Dried-Cherry Sauce

Aromatic jasmine rice cooks to a moist texture, which makes for perfect rice pudding. Use a pan with a heavy bottom to prevent scorching.

7½ cups water, divided
1½ cups uncooked jasmine rice
 1 teaspoon kosher salt
 1 (3-inch) cinnamon stick
 3 cups 2% reduced-fat milk
 ½ cup plus 2 tablespoons sugar, divided
 1 teaspoon ground cinnamon
1½ teaspoons vanilla extract, divided
 ¾ teaspoon almond extract, divided
 1 cup dried tart cherries
 1 tablespoon water
 1 teaspoon cornstarch

1. Combine 6 cups water and next 3 ingredients in a large, heavy saucepan; bring to a boil. Reduce heat, and simmer, uncovered, 20 minutes or until rice is tender. Drain.

2. Return rice and cinnamon stick to pan; stir in milk, ½ cup sugar, and ground cinnamon. Bring to a simmer over medium heat, stirring constantly. Reduce heat to medium-low; cook 30 minutes or until thick, stirring frequently. Discard cinnamon stick. Remove from heat; stir in 1 teaspoon vanilla and ½ teaspoon almond extract.

3. Combine cherries and remaining 1½ cups water in a medium saucepan; bring to a boil. Reduce heat, and simmer 20 minutes. Stir in remaining 2 tablespoons sugar; cook 5 minutes. Combine 1 tablespoon water and cornstarch. Add to cherry mixture; bring to a boil. Cook 1 minute or until slightly thick, stirring constantly. Remove from heat; stir in remaining ½ teaspoon vanilla and remaining ¼ teaspoon almond extract. Serve pudding with sauce. **Yield: 8 servings (serving size: ¾ cup pudding and about 2½ tablespoons sauce).**

CALORIES 290; FAT 2.1g (sat 1.1g, mono 0.5g, poly 0.1g); PROTEIN 6.2g; CARB 61.4g; FIBER 1.2g; CHOL 7mg; IRON 1.1mg; SODIUM 126mg; CALC 127mg

Chocolate Mousse

{Check for **Gluten**}

¾ cup semisweet chocolate
  chips, melted
1 (12.3-ounce) package reduced-
  fat extra-firm tofu
¼ teaspoon salt
3 large egg whites
½ cup sugar
¼ cup water
Frozen fat-free whipped topping,
  thawed (optional)
Grated chocolate (optional)

1. Place chocolate chips and tofu in a food processor or blender, and process 2 minutes or until smooth.

2. Place salt and egg whites in a medium bowl, and beat with a mixer at high speed until stiff peaks form. Combine sugar and ¼ cup water in a small saucepan; bring to a boil. Cook, without stirring, until candy thermometer registers 238°. Pour the hot sugar syrup in a thin stream over egg white mixture, beating at high speed. Gently stir one-fourth of meringue into the tofu mixture; gently fold in remaining meringue. Spoon ½ cup mousse into each of 8 (6-ounce) custard cups. Cover and chill at least 4 hours. Garnish with whipped topping and grated chocolate, if desired. **Yield: 8 servings.**

CALORIES 147; FAT 5.6g (sat 3.3g, mono 1.8g, poly 0.5g); PROTEIN 5.2g; CARB 22.5g; FIBER 0.2g; CHOL 0mg; IRON 0.9mg; SODIUM 134mg; CALC 26mg

Cooking Tip

Tofu is the key to making this dessert light and creamy, but you won't be able to taste it. Be sure to use plain tofu for the best results.

Minty Peach Sorbet

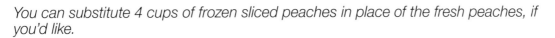

☑ Dairy **free**

You can substitute 4 cups of frozen sliced peaches in place of the fresh peaches, if you'd like.

4 cups chopped peeled peaches (about 2 pounds)
1 cup water
½ cup sugar
2 tablespoons fresh lime juice
2 (4-inch) mint sprigs, crushed

1. Combine all ingredients in a large saucepan; bring to a boil. Reduce heat, and simmer 7 minutes. Discard mint sprigs.

2. Place mixture in a blender or food processor; process until smooth. Pour into a bowl; cover and chill.

3. Pour chilled mixture into the freezer can of an ice-cream freezer; freeze according to manufacturer's instructions. **Yield: 8 servings (serving size: ½ cup).**

CALORIES 71; FAT 0.1g (sat 0g, mono 0g, poly 0g); PROTEIN 0.5g; CARB 18.5g; FIBER 1.2g; CHOL 0mg; IRON 0.1mg; SODIUM 0mg; CALC 4mg

Cooking Tip

Gently pressing or crushing the mint sprigs with a spoon releases the mint's fragrant oils and amps up the flavor in this sorbet. When buying fresh mint, look for bright green, crisp leaves with no signs of wilting. Fresh mint can also be frozen for later use. Simply rinse the leaves, pat dry, and freeze in a zip-top plastic freezer bag. The leaves will darken once they're frozen, but that won't affect the flavor. When you need to use some, just pull out what you need, and return the rest to the freezer.

Arctic Lime Freeze

 Dairy **free**

1 (12-ounce) can thawed limeade
   concentrate, undiluted
1 (12.3-ounce) package reduced-
   fat silken firm tofu, drained
1½ cups water
   Mint sprigs (optional)
   Grated lime rind (optional)

1. Place limeade and tofu in a blender; process until smooth. Add 1½ cups water; pulse to combine. Pour mixture into the freezer can of an ice-cream freezer; freeze according to manufacturer's instructions. Spoon the mixture into a freezer-safe container; cover and freeze 2 hours or until firm. Garnish with mint and rind, if desired. **Yield: 5 servings (serving size: 1 cup).**

CALORIES 196; FAT 3.1g (sat 0g, mono 0.7g, poly 1.7g); PROTEIN 7.8g; CARB 36.8g; FIBER 1.8g; CHOL 0mg; IRON 1.2mg; SODIUM 6mg; CALC 36mg

Cooking Tip

Making homemade ice cream, sorbets, and other frozen treats like this one at home is easy. You've got a couple of options when it comes to ice-cream makers: an old-fashioned bucket churn or a countertop freezer. Traditional bucket-style freezers require rock salt and ice, but tabletop models rely strictly on a freezer bowl filled with coolant.

Nutritional Analysis

How to use it and why

Glance at the end of any *Cooking Light* recipe, and you'll see how committed we are to helping you make the best of today's light cooking. With chefs, registered dietitians, home economists, and a computer system that analyzes every ingredient we use, *Cooking Light* gives you authoritative dietary detail. We go to such lengths so you can see how our recipes fit into your healthful eating plan. If you're trying to lose weight, the calorie and fat figures will probably help most. But if you're keeping a close eye on the sodium, cholesterol, and saturated fat in your diet, we provide those numbers, too. And because many women don't get enough iron or calcium, we can help there as well. Finally, there's a fiber analysis for those of us who don't get enough roughage.

Here's a helpful guide to put our nutritional analysis numbers into perspective. Remember, one size doesn't fit all, so take your lifestyle, age, and circumstances into consideration when determining your nutrition needs. For example, pregnant or breast-feeding women need more protein, calories, and calcium. And women older than 50 need 1,200mg of calcium daily, which is 200mg more than the amount recommended for younger women. Go to mypyramid.gov for your own individualized plan.

We use these abbreviations in our nutritional analysis

sat	saturated fat	**CHOL**	cholesterol
mono	monounsaturated fat	**CALC**	calcium
poly	polyunsaturated fat	**g**	gram
CARB	carbohydrates	**mg**	milligram

Daily nutrition guide

	Women Ages 25 to 50	Women over 50	Men over 24
Calories	2,000	2,000 or less	2,700
Protein	50g	50g or less	63g
Fat	65g or less	65g or less	88g or less
Saturated Fat	20g or less	20g or less	27g or less
Carbohydrates	304g	304g	410g
Fiber	25g to 35g	25g to 35g	25g to 35g
Cholesterol	300mg or less	300mg or less	300mg or less
Iron	18mg	8mg	8mg
Sodium	2,300mg or less	1,500mg or less	2,300mg or less
Calcium	1,000mg	1,200mg	1,000mg

The nutritional values used in our calculations come from either The Food Processor, Version 8.9 (ESHA Research), or are provided by food manufacturers.

Metric Equivalents

The information in the following charts is provided to help cooks outside the United States successfully use the recipes in this book. All equivalents are approximate.

Cooking/oven temperatures

	Fahrenheit	Celsius	Gas Mark
Freeze Water	32° F	0° C	
Room Temp.	68° F	20° C	
Boil Water	212° F	100° C	
Bake	325° F	160° C	3
	350° F	180° C	4
	375° F	190° C	5
	400° F	200° C	6
	425° F	220° C	7
	450° F	230° C	8
Broil			Grill

Liquid ingredients by volume

¼ tsp	=	1 ml						
½ tsp	=	2 ml						
1 tsp	=	5 ml						
3 tsp	=	1 tbl	=	½ fl oz	=	15 ml		
2 tbls	=	⅛ cup	=	1 fl oz	=	30 ml		
4 tbls	=	¼ cup	=	2 fl oz	=	60 ml		
5⅓ tbls	=	⅓ cup	=	3 fl oz	=	80 ml		
8 tbls	=	½ cup	=	4 fl oz	=	120 ml		
10⅔ tbls	=	⅔ cup	=	5 fl oz	=	160 ml		
12 tbls	=	¾ cup	=	6 fl oz	=	180 ml		
16 tbls	=	1 cup	=	8 fl oz	=	240 ml		
1 pt	=	2 cups	=	16 fl oz	=	480 ml		
1 qt	=	4 cups	=	32 fl oz	=	960 ml		
				33 fl oz	=	1000 ml	=	1 l

Dry ingredients by weight

(To convert ounces to grams, multiply the number of ounces by 30.)

1 oz	=	¹⁄₁₆ lb	=	30 g
4 oz	=	¼ lb	=	120 g
8 oz	=	½ lb	=	240 g
12 oz	=	¾ lb	=	360 g
16 oz	=	1 lb	=	480 g

Length

(To convert inches to centimeters, multiply the number of inches by 2.5.)

1 in	=					2.5 cm	
6 in	=	½ ft			=	15 cm	
12 in	=	1 ft			=	30 cm	
36 in	=	3 ft	=	1 yd	=	90 cm	
40 in	=					100 cm	= 1m

Equivalents for different types of ingredients

Standard Cup	Fine Powder (ex. flour)	Grain (ex. rice)	Granular (ex. sugar)	Liquid Solids (ex. butter)	Liquid (ex. milk)
1	140 g	150 g	190 g	200 g	240 ml
¾	105 g	113 g	143 g	150 g	180 ml
⅔	93 g	100 g	125 g	133 g	160 ml
½	70 g	75 g	95 g	100 g	120 ml
⅓	47 g	50 g	63 g	67 g	80 ml
¼	35 g	38 g	48 g	50 g	60 ml
⅛	18 g	19 g	24 g	25 g	30 ml

Subject Index

Recipe Index